Foundations of Spirituality

The Human and the Holy:
A Systematic Approach

Carla Mae Streeter, OP

A Michael Glazier Book

LITURGICAL PRESS
Collegeville, Minnesota

www.litpress.org

To Tad, Bob,
Margaret, and Suzanne,
my mentors.

A Michael Glazier Book published by Liturgical Press

Cover design by Jodi Hendrickson. Cover image: Thinkstock.

Scripture texts in this work are taken from the *New Revised Standard Version Bible* © 1989, Division of Christian Education of the National Council of the Churches of Christ in the United States of America. Used by permission. All rights reserved.

Material based on Carla Mae Streeter, "What Is Spirituality?" *Review for Religious* 56:5 (September–October, 1997), © 1997, Jesuits of the Missouri Province, http://www .jesuitsmissouri.org/review/welcome.html. Used with permission.

Material based on Carla Mae Streeter, "Organism, Psyche, Spirit—Some Clarifications: Toward an Anthropological Framework for Working with the Neuro-Psycho-Sciences," in *Advances in Neuroscience: Implications for Christian Faith*, © 2003, Institute for Theological Encounter with Science and Technology (ITEST), 20 Archbishop May Drive, St. Louis, MO, 63119, http://www.ITEST-faithscience.org. Used with permission.

Excerpts from Catherine of Siena, *The Dialogue*, trans. Suzanne Noffke, OP (New York: Paulist, 1980) © 1980, Paulist Press Inc., 997 Macarthur Blvd., Mahwah, NJ, 07430. Used with permission.

1   2   3   4   5   6   7   8   9

Library of Congress Cataloging-in-Publication Data

Streeter, Carla Mae.
    Foundations of spirituality : the human and the holy : a systematic
approach / Carla Mae Streeter.
        p. cm.
    "A Michael Glazier book."
    Includes bibliographical references and index.
    ISBN 978-0-8146-8071-1 — ISBN 978-0-8146-8096-4 (ebook)
    1. Spirituality.   I. Title.
    BV4501.3.S777   2013
    248—dc23   2012035878

Imagine a circle traced on the ground,

and in its center a tree sprouting. . . .

So think of yourself as a tree

made for love and living only by love. . . .

The circle in which this tree's root, your love,

must grow is true knowledge of yourself,

knowledge that is joined to me,

      God,

who like the circle have neither beginning nor end.

You can go round and round within this circle,

finding neither end nor beginning,

yet never leaving the circle.

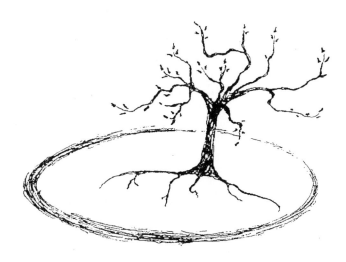

—Catherine of Siena, *The Dialogue* (New York: Paulist, 1980), 41.
Drawing and translation by Suzanne Noffke, OP.

Contents

Acknowledgments

As this study appears in written form, I am indebted to a cloud of witnesses who have each been a part of its formation, even if unawares. Back in 1979 I took a course at Regis College of the Toronto School of Theology that planted the seed. Taught by Tad Dunne, SJ, this early Foundations of Spirituality course was my introduction to the intentionality analysis of Bernard Lonergan, and from this analysis things began to unfold. This introduction was followed by a course in religion and culture taught by Bob Doran, SJ, in which I was introduced to the marvel of the human psyche and its significance in human healing and development. Frederick Crowe, SJ, and Tibor Horvath, SJ, guided me into doing a thesis on Lonergan's thought. During this time I lived under the watchful eye of Margaret Brennan, IHM, and it is to Margaret that I owe the prompting to do advanced degree work. I knew that if I did, its focus would eventually be the interface of psychological understanding with the dynamic of grace in the human person. Daniel Helminiak's work in psychology was an encouragement for me. Through the years we have mutually critiqued each other's work and challenged one another to more clarity. Suzanne Noffke, OP, the Catherinian scholar in my own Racine Dominican community, has affirmed my conviction that imagery can provide a rich loam for theological reflection, reinforcing my own conviction that sound thinking begins there.

I owe an immense debt to Kathleen Cour, OP, of the Springfield Dominicans, to Christine Cunningham, and to Michael Porterfield of Aquinas Institute for gifting me with their computer skills and creating diagrams on computer. To these I have named personally must be added the many students who have prevailed on me for years to do a text for the course they have taken and found so helpful.

Finally, I want to thank my colleagues who proofread and offered suggestions. What I offer here is tentative, but someone must make a first effort to take the rich insights of classical virtue theory and ground them in what empirical observation and present psychological understanding offer us. This is a first effort. I trust others will be forthcoming, and from this combined richness all of us can benefit.

Carla Mae Streeter, OP
Aquinas Institute of Theology
St. Louis, Missouri
2012, Fiftieth Anniversary of the Second Vatican Council

What Is Spirituality?

It's no secret—the search is on. TV talk shows, the *New York Times'* best-seller book lists, enneagram workshops—spirituality is *in*. Why does this topic hold such a fascination for us? Do we have a hunch that this thing called "spirituality" may be key to the healing of our American soul? What is it we are looking for? What *is* spirituality?

America is home to many faith traditions. Because we fear that any one tradition will take over our national soul (e.g., Islamophobia), we tend to privatize religion. In doing so, we domesticate it, relegating religion to our private lives, where it cannot be held publicly accountable. It is our own personal business. Because religion causes arguments, it is best left alone. But should it be? Religious traditions are one thing, but deep within them lies the heart of the matter. Churchgoer or not, deep within each human being radiates the spirituality that is mine just because I am a human being. I am a *spiritual* being. But what does this mean? How can we talk about it? It is spirituality that shines out from the lantern of any faith tradition on the lamp stand of home or business. It shines out or is cloaked even in the rejection of any faith tradition, for it is the spiritual person who is doing the rejecting.

What is this vital yet evasive reality? I suggest that the core of spirituality is the ache of human longing. We long for intimacy. We long to be connected with what matters, and so we make decisions to go after what we think will satisfy that longing. Frail as we are, we seek out intimacy with the Holy while being terrified it might consume us. We have a hunch that contact with the Holy will call us out of our pettiness

Much of the content of this introduction can be found in my article "What Is Spirituality?," *Review for Religious* 56:5 (September–October, 1997): 533–41, which can be accessed, along with the entire collection of *Review for Religious*, at http://www.jesuitsmissouri.org/review/welcome.html.

and self-interest, so deep down we fear it. But we long for intimacy with the human too. So pressing is this longing that we can manipulate and abuse each other in trying to satisfy it. Yet when we hurt, our hearts long to be comforted by a genuine caring presence, human or divine.

A Simple Definition

I propose that spirituality is *real presence*. It is being real, or fully human, and being really present—to myself, others, nature, the cosmos, the Divine. Said rather tritely, it is being *all there* wherever *there* happens to be. Someone's spirituality is the tone he or she brings when entering a room, an encounter, a project, a relationship. It is the summation of what we call sensitivity, intelligence, character, personality, human development, holiness, approach, social skills, or the lack of any or all of these, depending on maturity. Spirituality cannot be reduced to any of these any more than our presence can be reduced to our psychology, religion, or interpersonal skills. Spirituality is the tone of the self. Its beauty is being really *real*, genuinely present to any person or event in which I find myself. By its very nature, even if I don't intend it, this innate spirituality of mine points to the Holy. It is something pointing beyond my human limits, something transcendent, even if I reject the existence of such a reality.

The gift of real presence is received from another. When did you last receive it? Was it when you held your new smiling grandchild for the first time and said those wonderfully silly things grandparents say to new babies? Did it come to you at the precise moment when that little round face broke into a toothless grin? Maybe it was when your husband held you and let you cry when word came that your dad had breathed his last. Or maybe it was the way the love of your life took your face in her hands and kissed your eyes.

How can we tell if we're really *all there*? Someone who is really present is very attentive to people and to things going on. They are *with it*. They notice things. Then they begin wondering about them. They ask good questions, not questions that are smart-alecky or manipulative. They want the facts, the truth about what is going on around them. Once they know, they take a stand based on careful judgments or conclusions they have reached. They have opinions about things, and strong convictions. People who are really present are not *closed*. If you give them new data, they will consider changing their opinion, respecting the new truth offered them—but they will do so carefully.

Then these folks act. They move on what they know. They live out their convictions, in contrast to folks who might know a lot but do little about it. Finally, folks who are really present are people in love. They have been grasped by love, human or divine, and it makes them different. People who are in love are different from those who are not. People who are religiously in love move with respect on the earth and among people. They experience a longing for what is just, what is good, what is true, and what is holy. Their spiritual hunger is similar to a starving person in search of food.

Each religious tradition clothes this kind of presence with its own distinct manifestations. For Christians, the presence they bring to the human community is garbed in Christic homespun. Jesus of Nazareth is the text from which we come to know what God is really like and what we are to be like in relation to this Mystery. From his real presence among us historically we learn to be authentically *communal*, genuinely *incarnational*, and enamored of the *sacramental* nature of all of creation. These three publicly observable characteristics signal the identity of mainline Christians of various denominations worldwide. The proportion of these characteristics varies with differing denominations, due in large part to history and belief.

The *communal* nature of Christianity reveals a *we*-consciousness over and above a *me*-consciousness. Christianity shares this characteristic with the Judaic and Islamic traditions, the other two Religions of the Book, but the Christian lens will interpret its distinct communal identity with specific language: *unity in the risen Christ through the power of the Holy Spirit*. This communal characteristic is a counter-check on a rugged individualism.

The *incarnational* characteristic of Christian presence in the world will show itself publicly through an insistence that the human be taken very seriously in its free response to the Divine. Because the Holy wedded itself to humanness in the person of Christ Jesus, the Christian learns that the Holy will be found in the human as a partner for the healing of the world. As a result, a genuine Christian spirituality will need to deal seriously with human brokenness, abuse, and oppression. This incarnational aspect of Christian spirituality, when properly understood and taken seriously, prevents an escape into pietism and the "grin and bear it" posture of a pie-in-the-sky religiosity.

The *sacramental* aspect of Christian spirituality or presence is a direct outcome of the communal and incarnational characteristics. Because we are communal and in touch with the human, we discover that we are bonded to the entire cosmos and to the very heart of matter. As science continues to reveal the interconnectedness of all of matter, this discovery enhances the sacramental characteristic of Christian spirituality in a very deep way. The sacramental sense begins with all of created reality. Matter is revelatory of the Holy. As revelatory, it is a source of joy and celebration. From this realization comes worship in its various forms in the Christian community. Among some Christians this celebration is quite reserved and muted; among others it is exuberant and rich. Sacraments reveal a love affair with the earth, with smells and bells, water and oil, incense and salt, candles and color. Christians cannot shake the marvel of the marriage of God with humanness in the incarnation or ignore the fact that DNA and all the elements of the periodic table have had a part to play in the wedding.

Taking the Human Seriously

Even though spirituality can manifest itself in distinct religious ways, it shows itself mainly in the ordinary ebb and flow of everyday life. It walks around in jeans and sunglasses. It shows up at the bank, the supermarket, and the board meeting. It is what being human is all about. The human being is a marvel of biology. Unfortunately, we think about our biological *organism* most when we go to the doctor because something isn't working right. But we are far more than physicality. We have a *psyche*.

The human psyche is not a *thing* or a *part* of being human. It is an energy field that permeates our physicality and what we will identify as our distinctly human *spirit*. We are a bundle of psychic energy. This energy is more and more understood today through the science of psychology. It is a vital *life force* that orchestrates our cell division, our metabolism, and our mental health. In addition to being pure energy, it takes the form of emotion, imaging, fantasy, and imagination.

Psychic energy can take the form of powerful *motors* we call emotions. These motors are revved up by our psychic capacity to image things, to fantasize and imagine. This energy field is deeply seated throughout our physical organism through our neurological system. The psyche draws from our physical sensations and experiences, is the seat of deep feeling and affectivity, and has everything to do with the tone of our spirituality. In the usual triad of *body, mind, and spirit*, it is sorely neglected until, unfortunately, we may need clinical therapy. The psyche and its energy field are shared to a great extent with the animal realm. Yet there is still more to being human than biology and psychology.

If the psychic dimension of the human is shared in common with many animals, what really makes us distinctly human? We are obviously more than our emotions and our imaginations. What precisely are the functions of the human *spirit*? The human spirit operates in ways we can identify as more specifically *spiritual* rather than merely *psychic*. Again, function holds the clues to the distinctions we need. The human spirit has the capacity to *question*. We might say, then, that questioning is one of the most basic spiritual functions. We ask questions about our health, our house, the car, the cat, the children. Questions pop up about the Holy. I want to know how this One relates to me and those I love. We might say that the capacity to wonder, to inquire, to question, to want to know, as well as our awareness of wanting to know, is evidence of something more than raw psychic energy. It is empirical evidence for the distinct operations of the human spirit. But there is more.

We are most human by our capacity to *think* and *choose*. To think, we need to draw from the data of our senses and from the data that consciousness stores and presents us and that a psychic feeling memory preserves for us. When we are *conscious* we become *aware* of all this data. We question data to arrive at an understanding of it. We then question whether our understanding of it is true or not. Once we intelligently question and settle on answers, psychic energy with its images and emotions comes flooding back into consciousness. It influences us. We weigh what, if anything, we intend to do about what we know. Motivated, we lean toward a decision in line with our values. This activity also reveals further functions of the human spirit: spiritual activity. In the past we called it "evaluating" or "willing." We decide and we choose. Then we do this or that. Or if we are not attending to our emotions and not asking enough questions, we arrive at half-truth conclusions and make decisions that ruin our lives, injure ourselves or others, or make us look ridiculous. These operations—attentive awareness and wonder, questioning for understanding, judging the facts, and deciding—are the distinct functions of the human spirit. As far as we know, our pets do not function in this way. It will be these operations, then, that the Holy will be aiming at to influence and deal with us in the context of our human freedom. We provide an X factor. The Holy will engage us no matter how we fill that in.

These distinctions provide a certain new clarity about what we mean by the human *soul*. When I use the term "body," I will mean the *physical and psychic functions* operating in the human person. By "soul" I will mean *psychic energy plus evidence of the distinct functions of the human spirit*. When psychic energy is operating biologically, it directs my digestion. When it operates emotionally, it curbs my anger. When psychic energy becomes conscious in the operations of experiencing, understanding, judging, and deciding, we have soul activity. This is what is distinctly human, and it is this human that either is or is not in relation to the Divine.

The relationship of the human to the Holy is what I will mean by the term "holiness." Such a relationship can be implicit or explicit. Human is what we are. We may either be intentionally in relationship with the Mystery that is beyond ourselves or choose to ignore it. Whichever we choose, it is the human in its totality, *organism, psyche, and spirit*, that will do the choosing. This choice will contribute to the type of human presence we are identifying with spirituality. One's spirituality will be undeveloped, developing, or mature. This will be real regardless of one's chosen religion and despite any amount of denial. Clarifying these terms, even redefining them, will enable us to take the human quite seriously as we make day-to-day choices. Then we will be ready to consider spirituality as the distinct human presence brought to our relationship with the Holy in the unique tradition we identify as Christian.

When God Comes Courting

Wondrous is the human being that the Holy woos into holiness. Holy or not, the human is still spiritual because it functions spiritually, even if in defiance of God. But when the total human enters into relationship with God, we can expect the goose bumps intimacy brings. Holy women and men are embodied spirits who are in love with God. They have been grasped by divine Love and want to know what to do and what not to do. They are first of all in a *relationship*. Then they often seek out others to travel with, and Christians call this community of pilgrims "church."

This text will reflect on how the Holy comes to meet the human, or said another way, how the Holy works with this physical, psychic, and spiritual person. God works with precisely what God has made, enhancing it rather than overriding or disposing of it. The basic premise of this book is that every person is called to holiness. Holiness comes about through the relationship of the human with the Divine. Holiness is a divine summons heard and responded to by a *human* being.

This relating will involve physical, psychic, and spiritual response. So far we have paid attention to the human partner in this relationship. We have named the dimensions of the human as physical, psychic, and spiritual. What can we say of the Divine?

How does God engage the human? To search this out, Christians begin by watching Jesus of Nazareth. We watch the one in whom the human/divine union was complete, and we are amazed. To our surprise, his humanness is whole, complete, beautiful, and transformed in what we have come to know as *resurrection*—all of this is a result of contact with the Divine. This "show and tell" is important for us. It calms our fears about getting too close to God. Humanity has had a clear fear in history that if we get too close to God, we will be destroyed. In the man Jesus we are shown that humanness touched by God ends up being *transformed*, not destroyed.

The history of spirituality and the lives of mystics and theologians have much to tell those who study spirituality. Their lives reveal experiences, and some even try to talk about what they have experienced. Account after account reveals the Holy approaching the human like a beggar, hat in hand. There is a knock on the door of the heart. If the human so much as inquires, the Holy, present always at the depth of the soul and keeping the human in existence, enters into conscious awareness. It is one thing to be sustained by God and quite another *to become aware* that this Holy One has come calling, seeking a relationship. Religious experience influences our perspective. The presence of the Holy has entered our horizon of awareness. Our horizon has been changed, and the Guest becomes a reference for choice and behavior. We question and seek to understand what has happened. Religious conversion has begun, and for such a person God can no longer be ignored or shooed off like a pesky fly. God stands at the door of the soul and waits. This self-gift of God in friendship and mercy is called grace.

Transformation of the Human

The Divine comes bearing gifts. For the psyche there is longing now for nothing less than God. The object of the psychic emotion of hope is now nothing less than the Divine. What is now the *theological virtue of hope* builds on our psychic emotion of hope. Theological hope is a desire, an ache born of divine Love, that transforms human longing, stopping now at nothing less than God. Its source and object, *the Father* at the heart of the triune Mystery, is the hiddenness of God from which the longing springs. A knowing born of the same divine Love transforms the understanding and judgment. Such knowing, coming from loving, is called *faith*, and its source and object is the Divine revealing itself in the Word, from whence it comes. Rooted now in the Father, with the capacity to know now enlightened by the Word, the human also is given the capacity to evaluate and choose out of the very love that is at the heart of God. The Spirit's gift is *charity*, that active, dynamic, self-giving love that catches up the human emotion of love and changes its final goal. It now settles for nothing less than God. These three powers for human activity, called "theological virtues," seed the human with capacities beautiful to see in action. The change we call "conversion" has begun.

The change has immediate results on how one makes choices. *Moral* conversion is a shift from choosing short-term satisfaction to making choices based on long-term good. Our circle of concern expands beyond the usual self-interest. *Psychic* conversion may appear. It begins to dissolve the scar tissue of the psyche, the result of trauma and stored-up pain. Love can call us from this bondage, and therapy is often the scissors that cut the dead scar tissue away. Religious, moral, and psychic conversion—the Holy, like some housekeeper with a one-track mind, cleans out the human temple and begins the healing that will make its presence in the world different.

The most difficult change of all comes in knowing oneself—knowing one has not been attentive or intelligent in asking sufficient questions and as a result has arrived at rash judgments and regrettable decisions. Knowing how one's own consciousness works is *intellectual* conversion, and it is a far cry from replacing a few pieces of conceptual furniture. It is knowing how one knows and when one doesn't. This conversion means being aware of my awareness, understanding what it means to understand, and knowing how my judgment settles which understanding is correct. It means listening to my own emotions and how they influence my choices to act or not to act. Intellectual conversion is taking stock of the operations of my human spirit and coming to know how to cooperate in the building up of my own soul. Intellectual conversion puts us in charge of our own house. It calls us to accountability for our own human operations or for our own neglect of them to settle for acting less than human. It is an authentic self-knowledge and does not come cheaply. To engage it, one needs to make one's own interiority the object of evaluation. It is self-initiated interior accountability. Once admitted into consciousness, the presence of the Holy will do exactly what that presence did for Jesus in his humanness: bring it to utter fullness, completion, and beauty.

How do we know this is happening? We know because there is *evidence*. This evidence appears as repeated patterns of human behavior begin to manifest themselves. We call these patterns "virtues." We have already identified the first three: faith, hope, and charity. Believing, hoping, and loving transform the very *nature of the human*, orienting it to the Divine. As the human begins to act out of this new orientation, qualities begin to show in the humanness itself. Four qualities begin to show up in the ordinary ebb and flow of daily living. Their classic names are "prudence," "justice," "fortitude," and "temperance." Called "cardinal moral virtues," their object is the beautiful, balanced, functioning human being in its own right, informed by a gracious love.

Prudence is love's discretion. It marks the converted person as levelheaded, credible, and full of common sense; the person weighs the appropriateness of thinking and acting in light of what has become a primary love. *Justice* is love's fairness. In all dealings with others, respect and consideration are shown as one would expect the same for oneself. As prudence sets the tone in the intelligence, so justice sets the tone in the capacity to choose. In the face of racism, sexism, nationalism, and the political and economic self-interest evident in the daily news, the just person will have nothing to do with behavior outside the aura of the primary love that now directs one's life. Injustice or oppression of others rouses one from silence to a healthy expression of indignation. *Fortitude* is love's courage. It prompts one to take risks whenever one's primary love is at stake. This most personal love, this relationship with the Holy, becomes the strong rudder, guiding the unflagging energy needed for human affairs in the face of the daily challenges that can wear us down and make us act small. *Temperance* is love's moderation. Its first goal is to temper the "skin hunger" that would have us give free rein to use another person for our own satisfaction. Temperance brings love's strong hand to the more physical aspects of human life. It draws the entire body into the service of love. The temperate person is wonderfully sensual, delighting in the beauty of the human form, a beautifully served meal, fine wine, lovely music, and the rich colors of a delicately designed room. He or she knows how to fill life with beauty and finds it everywhere.

As this study unfolds, other familiar subjects that have been a part of Christian spirituality will enter into the discussion. What are the *gifts of the Holy Spirit*? How do they differ from the theological and moral virtues so basic to conversion? What do we mean when we speak of the *fruits of the Spirit*? How do they differ from the gifts? What are *charisms*, and what place do they have in personal spiritual development and service to the Christian community? What place does *prayer* have, and what does it mean? What is the importance of *forgiveness*, so prominent in Christian calls to conversion? Finally, what are the *Beatitudes*, and where do they fit in this array of wonders the Divine works in the human heart?

Our goal is to catch a glimpse of a real presence in our world—yours and mine. We are human beings, made so by the Mystery that has formed us out of nothing but love. The full response we will examine will flesh out a spirituality that we will deliberately call "incarnational," a bonding of the human with the Holy that is pervasive and entire. The world is indeed in search of the *real thing.* As we walk among our family members, friends, or those struggling with illness and death, we can settle for no less.

CHAPTER ONE

The Context for a Study of Spirituality

Spirituality and the Sciences

Many are convinced we have lost our souls. Others hold that science has replaced our souls, like motors in machines. I'm going to side with neither. Instead, I'm going to pose a different consideration: *What in us is asking the question?* I propose it is our souls in search of meaning. I suggest the soul is alive and well. *What we need to do is rethink what it is*. If the real question is "What *is* the soul?" we are hard pressed today to explain what it is that we are talking about. For some it is a mysterious entity that pops in and out of the body in successive lives. For others it is a unique creation at conception, integral to each person, and thus the form of the transformed body after death.

As the *form* of the body, the soul, for Christians, is not complete without the body, for the body is its expression. In the past we believed that when the body died, the soul lived on somehow, somewhere, and there was the impression that the body would catch up with it later. We do not need to explore the classic Platonic or Aristotelian explanations

These reflections are an adaptation of a paper that appeared in the proceedings of the Institute for Theological Encounter with Science and Technology (ITEST) workshop on "Advances in Neuroscience: Implications for Christian Faith" (September 2002). It was published as "Organism, Psyche, Spirit—Some Clarifications: Toward an Anthropological Framework for Working with the Neuro-Psycho-Sciences," in *Advances in Neuroscience: Implications for Christian Faith* (St. Louis, MO: ITEST / Science Press, 2003), 51–71. It is used with permission.

1

of the human soul here. Rather, we want to inquire into *how* these ancient explanations have developed into nuanced understandings of the human being. Plato taught that souls preexist. Aristotle, adopted by Thomas Aquinas for use in his own anthropology, taught that the soul is the *form* of the body, and in humans that form is intelligent and capable of free choice. But what is this form of which we speak? What *is* the soul?

Today anyone who asks what the soul is can easily be dismissed. For some, psychology has disposed of the soul. Unless a clear place for the soul is presented in the total overall anthropology of the human being, the concept can be simply rejected. Where is it? What is it? What does it have to do with the brain? These are just some of the questions that arrive with the very mention of the word. Former classical answers can be given, but for many, their minds in this time of psychological exploration will press further: *Why* is that so? *How* is that so? For many *that* it is so is no longer enough. We want to know *how*. We need a new understanding of the meaning of a reality we consider constitutive of being human.

The question of the soul is only the beginning. From our Christian perspective other questions present themselves. What is distinctly human in what we discover about the soul? What does the Divine have to do with the soul? Is the soul natural or supernatural? Does it belong to us as humans, or is the soul something of God in us? What exactly happens when grace interpenetrates human consciousness, bringing with it the array of virtues we have named theological and moral? What really are grace and virtue? What is the meaning of the grace-human interaction? Is there even such an interaction, and if so, how do we account for it? We will attempt to address these questions. The emphasis as we begin will be on the anthropological, but the anthropological for the Christian is not complete without addressing its relation to the Divine. Why doesn't the old static concept we have had about the soul still work? Is there another way to think and speak about it? What is a more inclusive framework for understanding the human? Why is the conventional triad of *body, mind, and spirit* inadequate? Is our suggestion, that *organism, psyche, and spirit* replace this popular triad, more adequate? Why? Do we have to learn a new language to speak about what we have called the "human soul"? In this first chapter we will begin the exploration, asking the honest questions posed in our time. It is to the distinctness of this time in history and thought that we turn now in our exploration.

A Second Axial Shift?

We can trace the term "axial shift" to the German existentialist philosopher Karl Jaspers. In his work *The Origin and Goal of History*, Jaspers suggests there is an axis on which the whole of human history turns. Jaspers locates this shift or turn of human consciousness to the period between 800 and 200 BCE.[1] The period in history prior to this shift might be called the primal cosmological period. This earlier use of the term *cosmological* refers to the early dawn of consciousness when the human perceived itself as a pawn of nature. The frequent victims of flood, windstorm, fire, and earthquake, humans worshiped these elements in some primal sense, similar to taking out an insurance policy. This early self-awareness is caught artistically still today in some forms of Asian art. A majestic mountain, a magnificent tree meet the viewer's eye, and on closer look, a tiny figure can be detected climbing the mountain. Water, air, fire, and earth, the four basic elements, play a large part in creating a sense of the self as subservient to the unrestricted power of nature.

This primal cosmological self-awareness does not come to an abrupt end with the year 800 BCE. Like a new dawning, the axial shift occurs gradually. The shift is a new awareness, and it consists in the exciting possibility that with some thought, humans can harness the powers of nature. Science, in its most primitive form, is born. Where flooding occurs, we can build housing on stilts. Where we observe fire, we can tend and contain it; observe the wind, build structures designed to withstand its power; observe animals, notice how they warn of pending earthquakes.

In addition to this scientific shift, there is a *moral* shift. Ritual in its exactness and conformity ruled the early cosmological period. If the ceremonial was done carelessly, the gods might get angry, and the entire nation would be punished. With the axial shift a new awareness dawns: perhaps the gods are angry *because of the way I treated my wife last night*. This new moral sense influenced religious practice. Religions

---

[1] See Bernard Lonergan, *Collected Works of Bernard Lonergan*, vol. 4: *Collection*, ed. Frederick E. Crowe and Robert M. Doran (Toronto: University of Toronto Press, 1988), 237–38; and *A Second Collection*, ed. William F. J. Ryan and Bernard J. Tyrrell (London: Darton, Longman and Todd, 1974), 226–27. See also Karl Jaspers, *Origins and Goals of History* (New Haven, CT: Yale University Press, 1953), 26; and Arnold Toynbee, *Mankind and Mother Earth: A Narrative History of the World* (New York: Oxford University Press, 1976), 178.

became organized to not only guide the ritual practice of their devotees but to shape their behavior once they left the temple or shrine.

What is interesting to note in this history is that every major religion and philosophy takes early form during this axial shift across the globe. Confucius appears in China; Socrates, Plato, and Aristotle appear in Greece; the Jewish prophets arise in ancient Israel; Zoroaster appears in Persia. In India the Hindu sacrificial fire-worship rituals of the Vedas give way to the Upanishads and the Epics. The Buddha emerges, pointing to an interior focus rather than to the ritual emphasis found in Hinduism at his time. Formal religion and science then arise together with the shift in human consciousness to analytical thinking and the evaluation of action. Critical thought that seeks not only to describe but to *explain* is born.

Gathering momentum by 200 BCE, the *anthropological* shift places the human being and its capacity for inquiry at center stage. With each passing century, cosmic mythology recedes more and more into the background. The thinking human male becomes the measure of all things. All religions and cultures are brought gradually under human control sociologically, politically, and economically. The history of the West is the record of this shift from the influence of the cosmos with its mysterious gods and God. The power of the human mind finally achieves "enlightenment" between 1730 and 1780. Reason and science reign supreme. What cannot be observed or understood by the human mind is relegated to the ancient realm of myth and thus rendered inconsequential and childish. Religion itself comes under this critical eye, and faith is considered by some as immature, the evidence of a mind not yet come of age, not yet ruggedly free of its dependent relationship upon the God of one's childhood. Anthropological fixation on the human being seeks total independence and self-sufficiency, needing no one. For many, self-sufficiency and independence (not relationship and interdependence) become the epitome of what it means to be human.

In this self-absorption, rationalism and scientism reign supreme. For some the successes of the industrial age and the city-state with its political democracy or socialism become all the worship one needs. New technologies, so full of creativity and promise, are put into the service of a militarism the world had never imagined. Education aims at training minds to be scientifically sharp and efficient. The trained rational mind becomes the goal of state-sponsored education. Psychology is born as a new discipline, moving beyond the medical field into the realms of emotion, trauma, and mental illness. As a result of its

growing isolation, the human becomes more and more fragmented. The
brain takes control, and anything beyond the measurable is dismissed
as arbitrary and undependable. Empathy, affectivity, and compassion
recede into the cultural background.

In the late nineteenth century the Catholic Church in particular
reacted to this state of affairs both positively and negatively. On the
positive side, the great social encyclicals were written, sounding the
clear call for the recognition of workers' rights. Negatively, the church
regarded the shift to reason and self-sufficiency as a form of idolatry
and assumed a public position of entrenchment with a denouncement
of modern trends branded as "modernism." The extremities of anthropocentrism were grouped under this label of modernism and roundly
condemned. With this condemnation both the wheat and the weeds,
intertwined, came unavoidably under censure.

The twentieth century brought a time of shocking disenchantment
and disillusion. Unchecked rationalism and scientism revealed a tragic
underside. To the horror of the world, the two world wars revealed
to us starkly where an unethical technology could lead. The death
camps and Hiroshima and Nagasaki rose up as specters to haunt us.
With instant media coverage, the world saw the carnage of Vietnam
up close. A growing disgust with war was born. In the United States,
conscientious objectors fled to Canada and burned draft cards. The
ensuing years saw communism fall and the Berlin Wall crumble under
the urgency of those seeking peace. The human idols of rationalism and
scientism were showing they had clay feet, but there was no going back.
Science and technology were here to stay. The only way was forward,
using discernment and careful choice.

Some are convinced the worship of the mind has led to the loss of
the soul in a rudderless postmodern relativism. But others are sensing
that humankind is moving toward still-further development, that we are
indeed on the cusp of a *second* axial shift in consciousness. This new
cultural shift is again gradual, moving like a global thaw. The science
of psychology has ushered in a shift to philosophical interiority, the
exploration of the human subject in the intelligent operations of human
consciousness. Human self-awareness has become the object of exploration. With the birth and unfolding of neuroscience, new boundaries
have been crossed. The psychological sciences have begun to explore
human consciousness, and the psyche in its healthy and unhealthy
functioning has been the object of intense study. Psychology has also
become aware of a threshold it is not able to cross: there is a depth of

mystery in the human that its pragmatic testing cannot measure. The term "spiritual," until now used only in a religious context, began to be used in scientific parlance. Attention has turned to the exploration of *inner* space. Writers are suggesting that with this probing of the consciousness of the human subject, the second axial shift, the shift to *interiority*, has begun.

This new shift is not a return to the past, to the integrated medieval worldview of a unified sacred and secular. The shift to interiority is occasioned by desperation. It is prompted by the lonely howl of the human lost in the bottomless pit of its own limits. Crying for something more than human finitude, we stand like children looking in horror at our smashed images of God in a heap on the floor. The concepts of God as avenger, monarch, and autocrat are lying smashed by historians, cultural anthropologists, and even some theologians. Stripped of the old notions of Ultimate Reality and not fitted with new ones, many feel lost, orphaned, and alienated from the religious images they had known from childhood and have nothing secure with which to replace them. A vacuum begs to be filled. If the God we thought we knew is dead, what is there to replace this central ground, distorted as it may have been? Since science and technology with its weaponry can destroy us, what can save us? For some the solution is obvious: we must save ourselves. What is there besides our own minds? Our science? Our cleverness? Our self-indulgence? The conclusion may be rash, but we cannot overlook the fact that this honest questioning might hold hope of a rediscovery of the Mystery of the Holy in a way we have never known it. Is it possible that the *way inward* holds hope of a new and vital knowledge of who the human being really is?

What Kind of Interiority?

We might ask what leads philosophers and cultural anthropologists to believe this shift is actually taking place and whether it is global in its extent. One indicator is the interest today in *spirituality* even while there is a growing dissatisfaction with institutionalized religion. If bookstores are any indication, the spirituality section today covers everything from tarot card reading and the Enneagram to Hildegard of Bingen and the Zen mystics. Spirituality is a major section of interest in the store. Academically, in philosophy there has been a subtle shift to the consciousness philosophers, those who take the turn to the subject seriously and are showing that this turn need not result in

Kantian subjectivism. Although the term "interiority" has a religious ring for some, the use of the term here refers to a shift to *philosophic* interiority, or the understanding of how we function in our human consciousness.

It cannot be assumed that the human cry rising from postmodern fragmentation is consciously religious. It is, however, a cry of the lost, the disconnected. The cult of the human has become a confinement in that very humanness. The cry is a cry from prison. The openness to the transcendent afforded in the past by religion has been lost. What happens to us when there is nothing beyond ourselves to relate to? Where does one begin to find oneself in relation to something ultimate in this state of affairs? The postmodern position that there is no ultimate *anything* leaves many empty. Is there nothing beyond ourselves? The way to freedom begins *in the very questioning* of where we find ourselves. Our age has been prone to being blinded by our own human accomplishments to the point of self-worship. The way out will begin with a proper reassessment of that same humanness—the human in relationship to *all* of reality: the cosmos, nature and the earth, other human beings, and the Divine. This is no pouring of new wine into old skins. New skins must be prepared to hold the new wine.

The turn to interiority can be a finding of oneself in total truth. It can be a coming home. It will require a step, a turning, a *conversion* many fear to take. The way has been pointed out by the precursors, the consciousness philosophers. Writers such as Gadamer, Habermas, and Apel have challenged us with the task of attending to how human consciousness deals with reality. They warn us that worldviews will remain an eclectic smorgasbord until we have attended to how the mind processes data, how it arrives at conclusions. They wrestle with the fact that truth seeking can become infested with bias. They tell us *that* truth seeking must be done. They do not tell us *how the consciousness functions* in order to do it.

One group of scholars has taken steps into this new uncharted territory. Led by the Canadian Jesuit methodologist Bernard Lonergan, a small band of philosophers, economists, scientists, and theologians has begun an exploration into *interiority analysis*. Put in simple terms, they make the operations of their own intelligence the object of scrutiny. They offer a theory of cognition arrived at empirically through critical self-observation. They seek to give an answer to the question "What am I doing when I am knowing?" To clarify what knowing really is, they attempt to chart empirically the active intelligence-in-operation to determine its pattern of recurrent operations. Lonergan took his cue from his study of Aquinas. In question 84 of the *Summa*, Aquinas states that the intelligence can be known *only in its act*. Learning to attend to this action enables the thinker to arrive at *self-appropriation*, or a heightened awareness of whether one is authentically engaging the intelligence in all of its operations or selectively omitting some of those operations through bias. When this is done communally with others, mutual critique can bring about a high degree of accountability. The underlying premise in such activity is the conviction that real objectivity is arrived at only through authentic subjectivity.[2] Without the proper attention to the subject's operations, there can be no empirical accountability of how the intelligence is processing data. Discussion of "objectivity" without this can be illusory. Objective truth may be there, but the biased mind may never come to know it. Bias needs to be intelligently addressed and evaluated. Only with this kind of intentionality communally recognized can any level of accountability be claimed.

This shift to interiority calls for the *thematic objectification* of subjective operations. To thematize data is to put it in a conceptual form able to be scrutinized by others. The careful attentiveness to one's own conscious operations is new, and some dismiss the effort as obscurantist, labeling the scholars who attempt it as elite and obtuse. Incorrectly lumped with Transcendental Thomists,[3] the work of these scholars is dismissed by some philosophers, theologians, and scientists who are puzzled by this turn to the subject to make its conscious operations clear. Rather than referring to a mere change of mental concepts, the term refers to giving an account of the operations involved in *how one knows*. It is an analysis of how consciousness itself functions cognitively.

Lonergan Centers have sprung up in Toronto, Santa Clara, Milwaukee, Boston, Dublin, Naples, Sydney, Mexico City, Tokyo, Manila, and Rome. Learning *the method* means coming to know how one's own consciousness works. Analyzing one's own interiority requires focused attention on the empirical operations of the consciousness as it functions. The understanding of this functioning then becomes the

---

[2] See one example of Lonergan's discussion of this in *Method in Theology* (London: Darton, Longman and Todd, 1972), 265, 292.

[3] Lonergan has his own comments on the labeling resulting from this lack of understanding. In a footnote on pp. 13–14 of *Method in Theology*, he distinguishes his work from that of Transcendental Thomists such as Otto Muck (*The Transcendental Method* [New York: Herder and Herder, 1968]).

key to understanding the way the intelligence works, whether to plan a vacation or to research the human genome. If we can envision a group of scholars attending to this process together in order to verify and nuance it, we have some understanding of what Lonergan intended. What he intended was interdisciplinary scholarship based on an empirical observation of how humans work when they come to *know* anything. In other words, the approach to transforming human culture is grounded in attending to the *method* of actual empirical and intelligent human operation and in being accountable for its understandings, judgments, and decisions.

What Anthropology Is Needed?

The usual categories of rational psychology will no longer be adequate to this task. Drawn from Aristotelian and Thomistic theories of human nature, these theoretical categories, though many of their insights are valuable and true, cannot be the starting place. The starting place is in empirical observation of the functioning human being and in giving an account of what is going on when the human comes to know anything. Does the same thing happen again and again? Is there a pattern that repeats itself? Can the operations be recognized and named? If the answer to these questions is yes, we are on our way to *grounding* whatever theory of knowing we propose, in language the scientifically trained mind can understand with us. An empirically based cognitional theory would underpin our epistemology, allowing scientists and theologians to talk to one another about the human being from an observable base. From such an empirical base one would give an account of human operation any scientist could follow, while the theologian might be questioning the activity of grace in the heart of the same human. They draw from different *data*, one from empirical human functioning, and the other from the impact of revelation provided by faith. The functioning human uses the same consciousness for both, and accountability can be asked whether or not he or she is a believer in the religious sense.

Lonergan calls the empirical process needed to ground a sound cognitional theory "interiority analysis." It presupposes an accurate empirical charting of the operations of human cognition and identifies four main levels of operation: experience, understanding, judgment, and decision. The human operations that pertain to each of these levels are named, and a cyclic and recurrent pattern is charted. If Lonergan is on to something, a new meaning has been found for the old adage "Know thyself."

One way out of the sense of postmodern relativity would be to do an accountable self-appropriation. This means recognizing and naming one's own cognitive functions. This attentive awareness and careful scrutiny of one's own intellectual operations is necessary for the human to become accountable personally and communally in his or her search for the truth. Finding the full truth about the human would also mean the possibility of opening the human once again to its rightful place in the cosmos. This return would imply a reexamination of the *relationship* the human has with nature, with other human beings, and with the Divine. The truth needs to be sought without bias, but bias needs to be identified and named *communally*. Where does it function to block the operations of intelligence? But in addition to giving an account of how one reaches a judgment of truth, there will need to be an account of how we reach a judgment of *value*. It is value that motivates human choice. We need an anthropology that can adequately *explain how* we might address these questions.

The context of Western Christians has changed. As Christians we are no longer living in a cultural or religious ghetto. The media has opened us up to the reality of the global village. Considering an adequate anthropology for the work ahead of us requires that we see anthropology as pertaining to others as well as to ourselves. What do we find when we expand our horizon to a global perspective? We find that history and cultures have had much to do with the lenses we wear to try to understand.[4] In the past we have narrowly concluded that our lens is the only lens. Our expanding worldview teaches us quickly how inadequate this view is. Those working with interiority analysis are convinced that cultural difference is compatible with the basic operations of human consciousness. They suggest that these operations are human and thus cross-cultural; their outer manifestations, however, are distinct to the cultures in which people live.

Is it possible for us to do the work of interiority explicitly from a faith perspective? Can anthropology, as it opens up in interiority analysis, hold insights for the incarnation itself? For Christians this

---

[4] For some of the reflections that follow regarding energy and East/West contrasts, I am indebted to Gerald May, MD, *Will and Spirit: A Contemplative Psychology* (San Francisco: HarperSanFrancisco, 1982), chapter 7, pp. 172–209.

mystery is the bridge[5] reaching out to our humanness to connect us to the Divine. Work done in interiority analysis will impact not only our knowledge of ourselves but also our understanding of this central mystery. In what follows, we will be focusing on human anthropology using the approach of probing the intentionality operative in our human interiority. I want to make clear that the explorations into anthropology in what follows are not to be understood apart from this human-divine connection, even if at first we do not address the Divine directly.

If we are going to take the neurosciences seriously, for example, we are clearly addressing human anthropology. So, scientifically, where are we to begin? I suggest we begin with a very scientific term, the word "energy." Much has been written about energy as a life force because it occurs in all living things and indeed because its different forms are observed through space exploration.[6] But I would like to begin with a specific focused energy that, unlike light, electrical, and nuclear energy, has been researched very little. What is the nature of love's energy? Since our earlier question was about what makes humans fully human, we need to focus our sights on the most human of our energies, the energy of love. Like a *basso continuo*, love is the distinct energy that not only influences the full flourishing of the human but provides for us in the human world a bridge to the realm of transcendence.

In a recent article, *The Christian Science Monitor* announced just such a pursuit.[7] No longer satisfied with the "selfish gene" theory as the bottom line, scientists are undertaking an investigation into the nature of the energy of love and its expression. Alarmed by international violence and hate, bioethicist Stephen Post, who will head the new effort, believes we have no real alternative, considering the present state of the world. Reporter Jane Lampman claims the study reveals a shift within key disciplines from focusing on the negative in human

---

[5] This is the image given by God to Catherine of Siena in her *Dialogue*. I recommend searching the index (p. 376) for the multiple uses of this powerful image (Catherine of Siena, *The Dialogue*, trans. Suzanne Noffke, OP [New York: Paulist, 1980]).

[6] A recent work by an assistant professor of nursing in New York poses some interesting questions. The author, writing from a scientific point of view, is convinced that a careful study of energy will bring about the convergence of science and religion (Vidette Todaro-Franceschi, *The Enigma of Energy: Where Science and Religion Converge* [New York: Crossroad, 1999]).

[7] See Jane Lampman, "Scientists Put Love under the Microscope," *The Christian Science Monitor* 94:132 (June 3, 2002): 1 and 4.

nature to taking a hard look at what makes humans thrive. Located at a prominent medical school, Case Western Reserve University in Cleveland, the new Institute for Research on Unlimited Love begins its work with an initial endowment of four million dollars. The effort will engage disciplines from psychology and human development to public health and medicine, neuroscience, sociology, and evolutionary science. It will also explore the links between religion, spirituality, and human behavior. Why might this be of interest to us as scientists, as theologians, as spiritual guides?

Several traditions in both the East and the West hold that the different manifestations of love share a common ground of energy and that this common energy is the basic life force of the universe. Gerald May, MD, proposes that the different manifestations of love are expressions of a root spiritual energy that is *processed and differentiated* through the human psyche. May calls this root energy "agape" and likens it to a base metal, "irreducible and unadulterated." Taken as fragments of energy into the psyche, it becomes mixed with "certain aspects of self-definition" appearing "in conscious human experience."[8] Could it be that it runs on a type of created energy that has as its source an energy that is an unconditional type of loving? Would this energy have a relation to what we identify as the Divine? In this energy source, is *everything* divine, as some Eastern traditions suggest, but with the distinctions we in the West want to hold?

As Christians we believe that God is personified love and that this love is the source of all created reality. What might this have to do with this energy?

As hidden *source*, this love we call "God" is called "Father." This love expresses itself and so is also a "Word." This same love as God's active self-giving we call "Holy Spirit." We teach that Christians will be known by an agapic or self-giving love manifested in our behavior toward one another, and that this charity is a theological virtue created in the human soul to enable us to love with God's own love. Human love can become deformed, as May suggests. But when human love is interpenetrated with this divine energy as charity, there is a godly influence on our human loving. Can the dynamic agapic energy May is referring to as root cause be the uncreated Spirit of God as named by

---

[8] Gerald May, "Energy: The Unifying Force," in *Will and Spirit: A Contemplative Psychology* (San Francisco: HarperSanFrancisco, 1982): 172.

Christians? Does this *dynamis*, or active love, create in the human a conscious energy that can communicate and influence the wider world? Does the incarnation of the Word create a bridge for divine love to be in direct contact with the human through the sacred humanity of the Word? Is the human an instrumental cause of the transformation of human culture through the energy of love?

In both Eastern and Western thought frames, energy of some kind is fundamental to being. Western physics sets itself to find a unified field theory that could identify all creation as energy. May states that for Freud it is libido arising from the "biological substrata" of the id, the anatomical and physiological foundations of unconscious motivation. W. R. D. Fairbairn, in contrast, holds the "object relations" theory of personality. Here the ego has its own intrinsic energy, also called "libido." Behavioral psychology views psychic energy as the simple physical product of cellular oxidation. Most Western theories presuppose that psychic energy originates in and is limited to the individual human brain and body.[9]

The East, and Asian thought in particular, does not make a distinction between psychology and spirituality. As a result, the East poses the existence of a universal energy that manifests itself mentally and spiritually in people and also in the physical workings of the cosmos as a whole. Known as *chi* in China, *ki* in Japan, *sakti* or *kundalini* in Sanskrit, this universal energy is understood to be manifested everywhere and not to be limited to expression in human consciousness. This energy is understood as a basic universal life force, undetermined and ambiguous in itself.

Western thought, shaped by the rational and scientific approaches of the Enlightenment, identifies the *human as the origin* of this energy. The East, its insights flowing from more contemplative traditions, maintains that whatever the physiological point of origin might be, the energy manifested in consciousness originates first as raw, undifferentiated energy *outside of the human*. Rather than settle for the ambiguity of the Far East or the anthropocentrism of the West, the Christian suggests yet another option. Could it be that the power of God *creates* life energy in the universe, each creature manifesting an energy proper to its being? Why is it important to clarify these viewpoints? The role of

---

[9] May holds that even Jung in his reference to the collective unconscious understands psychic energy as originating in the human. See May, *Will and Spirit*, 341n7. For the comparison of Eastern/Western points of view, see ibid., 173–77.

the human must be given its due, neither deified nor dismissed, and the *relationship* of the Divine to the human in its operations needs to be clarified. The Christian position is a *both/and*, not an *either/or*, solution. The human functions as human, and that functioning provides the data science needs. The Divine relates to the human as source of life and creator of human energy. The relationship is one of the empowerment of what is already there, not its replacement. This is the clarification we need in order to take a position on the functioning of the prime center of human consciousness as it expresses itself, the human brain.

As Christians we hold that the parts of the human brain that seem to generate certain emotions[10] are really acting as filters or suppressors of the psychic energy belonging innately to human beings. If this is possible, then the anatomical brain locations where emotion seems to originate are not actually the *generators* of the emotion but are merely the places where emotional energy is *mediated* into awareness. Neurochemical processes, then, would not be the source of emotional energy but would act instead as custom-designed filters, changing the energy's form and expression. The brain is a physical organ, a neurological network of synapses. The mind, however, refers to the spiritual capacity of the human to *sublate* or transpose brain events as a network of attentive, intelligent, reasonable, responsible, and loving events. In a respectful stance, this clarification might allow theology and science to converse and share insights.

A New Look at Humanness

Rethinking Human Anthropology

To suggest an anthropology more suited to this task, it becomes essential to ask what the basic dimensions of the human might be. Science in its exploration of the human genome has much to tell us of our physicality. Psychology and psychiatry continue to explore the marvel of the human psyche. Can we use interiority analysis to be more precise about what the human spirit is? Can we attempt to chart the anatomy of the human spirit? Is the human spirit synonymous with the soul? Is the human spirit natural or supernatural? What is the human spirit's relationship to the psyche? These are wonderful questions beg-

---

[10] See, e.g., the work of Candace Pert in *Molecules of Emotion* (New York: Scribner, 1997).

ging honest answers. The description of the human in popular jargon is "body, mind, and spirit." Is this adequate? Where are the emotions in such a description? What does each of the three words in the pop culture description refer to? With these questions before us, we will begin our exploration with a revised anthropology as the basis of the anthropological foundations of spirituality.

A Revised Anthropology

Returning to our starting point with energy, note first that the human being manifests energy in a distinctly human way. Most visible to the eye, our DNA takes form in what we will call the human "organism." This dimension of ourselves is known not only by its visibility but by its distinct functions. The organism consists of a complexity of systems. We can identify many of these systems: circulatory, respiratory, lymphatic, digestive, reproductive, neurological, and so forth. The wonder of the function of the human organism is coming to the fore as science daily probes deeper into its intricacies. In keeping with our conviction that the human is grounded in the heart of God, the organism mediates the created energy proper to itself while remaining grounded in that creative power.

The example of the application of this faith conviction in classic theology is an understanding of God as the One who *is*. This Mystery, in which essence and existence are one, is said to bestow *being* on all creatures so that they can *be*. This would mean that the One who is, God, uses the ovum and sperm of our parents as instrumental causes to bring us to *be*. Their physicality, manifesting the energy of their human love and desire, enters into partnership with the Divine to cause another to *be*. In classical terminology, this is the primary efficient cause, God, creating in and through instrumental causes, namely, our parents.

Human consciousness, as it emerges from childhood awareness to a more mature self-reflection, begins to attend to two sources of data. The most common database for us is the data of sense provided through the human organism. We touch, smell, hear, taste, and see. By our five senses we glean information from our environment and surroundings. The second source of data is more subtle. It is the data of consciousness itself. As we grow, we become more and more *aware* that we are touching, smelling, hearing, tasting, and seeing.

By *attentiveness* we notice things. We attend to what our senses or consciousness is calling to our attention. We are attentive to external data and to consciousness itself as simple *experience*. This primary experiential level is the level of awe, the simple contemplative experience of wonder—at the beauty of a sunset, at the face of a child, at the mystery of God. Lest this level of operation be quickly dismissed, I propose that it opens us to that mysterious psychic energy field that is the object of the psychological sciences. The *psyche* is the unconscious repository of sensitive feeling memories. From it spring dreams, imagining, and fantasy. It is in the hidden depths of the psyche that energy mysteriously gathers in intensity to be manifested as the eleven powerful human emotions.

A careful distinction needs to be made here. Psychic energy becomes *conscious* at what we will identify as the first level of the human spirit, that of experience. What this implies is that psychic energy is real but sometimes not noticed. It is *unconscious*. When we become aware of it, we speak of being *conscious* of it. This first level of conscious awareness is psychic energy functioning as the first level of the distinctive human *spirit*. The psyche is an energy field that stores the data of sense from physical functioning and also stores the data of consciousness from what will be going on in the operations of the human spirit. The psyche is thus distinct from the human spirit but not separate from it, distinct from the organism but not separate from it. It becomes important for us to identify the operations that belong not only to this first level of consciousness but to all the levels of the human spirit. Once we do this, we may be able to redefine what we mean by the *soul* with some reference to distinctive human function.

If the awareness of human experience identifies the first level of conscious operation, what drives the energy of the human spirit forward? I am going to suggest that it is *drawn forward*, that it is *lured*. The human spirit is curious. As if drawn by an unseen undercurrent, the consciousness longs to find out; it desires to understand. From first-level, simple awareness it moves to a new set of operations marked by *inquiry*. Questions emerge. Why is the sky that reddish color tonight? Why didn't my husband come home? Why was I born? This second level of the human spirit is known by its *questioning for understanding*. Relentless in its probing, the consciousness searches through questioning. Its inquiry leads to "Aha!" moments when bits of images connect into insights, and insights fuse to form concepts, and concepts fuse to form ideas.

The consciousness shifts again in its empirical operations as we identify a third level of operation. The questions change. Are my bright ideas *right* ideas? Am I onto what is really true? Have I reached the truth of what really is? The consciousness, like a laser, scans all the insights gathered. If no further questions present themselves, a tentative conclusion is made and a *judgment of the truth* of the matter is reached. In a court case the prosecuting attorney presents the evidence and questions the defendant. The jury considers the facts. A *judgment* is then made by the jury, and it is the judge who executes the judgment. What is crucial in tracing intentionality is the realization that knowing is reached only at the point of judgment, not at the levels of experience or inquiry. Knowing consists of three functions: attentiveness to data, inquiry for understanding, and the judgment that the understanding is correct. But the human spirit is not only made for knowing. It is made for decision and action. The human spirit has a fourth level of operation.

Again the psychic energy, now conscious, shifts in its operations. As though choreographed by some unseen dance coach, a new form of questioning emerges. This time it is not a question of fact, of truth. (We have already discovered the facts in the judgment, and until new data should appear and the pattern sets about repeating itself, the judgment arrived at becomes our position.) The question now becomes, what difference does it make? What's it worth to you? Knowledge of the facts is one thing. Value is another. Back to the court scene. How will amends be made for this crime? What is a fitting penalty? A judgment of *value* is sought. The human spirit is moving into the level of *evaluation*, and it is from value, from worth, that the human makes a choice. This final level of human operation, the fourth, is the level where *willing* goes on. It is the level of responsible choice, decision, and action.

A Functional Perspective

Charting our intentionality offers us a *functional* explanation of the operations of the human spirit. Why is this important, and what will it mean to a study of spirituality? It is important because function is empirical and the scientific mind cannot disregard it. Empirical function is the doorway through which the human can be explored psychologically, socially, and spiritually, as well as religiously. Interiority analysis suggests that consciousness functions differently through identifiable sets of human operations. These operations clarify what human *knowing* really is and when it is reached, and what human *willing* is and when we are engaged in it. Perhaps most of all, the *self-appropriation* that results from charting our intentionality reveals what a developed *conscience* actually is—a human consciousness operating on the fourth level of operation and aware that it is responsible for the choices it makes. We may begin to understand better what "having full knowledge and full choice" might really mean regarding moral responsibility.

With this bare sketch, we can now sum up the anthropology we have begun. The human consists of an *organism* made up of complex systems that are mutually interdependent. The human consists of a powerful *psychic energy field*, which stores images, releases those images in dreams, and releases emotions when these "energy motors" are aroused through the functions of the organism or the operations of the human spirit. The human consists of a distinctly *human spirit* with levels of operation that can be empirically identified as "experiencing," "understanding," "judging," and "deciding." The human organism, plus the psychic energy that pulsates within it, is what we are defining here as "body." The human spirit, with its operations of knowing and choosing plus the psychic energy that becomes conscious in these operations, is what we will identify as "soul." Psychic energy is present in both the bodily organism and the human spirit, acting as a bridge and a unifier. The human is a composite of spirit and matter. We are an embodied spirit, a spiritual embodiment.

The Soul as Measure of the Culture

In the not too distant past, the Christian researcher too quickly damned the scientific and rational viewpoint as destructive of faith. Those wiser knew better than to disclaim science and reason. The marvel of the human spirit and its search for the facts calls us to seek the truth—the real as known by the mind. The science of the brain must be given its full due. What does this mean? For one thing, it means that neurological and brain science must be taken seriously. For another, sound self-appropriation that reclaims the contemplative wonder in our awareness needs to be taken just as seriously. We have before us a challenge. The false dichotomy between science and spirituality/ religion needs to be laid to rest, and effort must be made to push the questions until they yield both scientific and theological truth. One or the other is no longer enough. The brain is not the mind. The brain is the mind's physiological infrastructure.

There is no magic "how to" to this project. Nor does it depend on some "facts out there." If the operations of the subject, the thinker, are not attended to, there remains only a potpourri of viewpoints with little or no accountability. Truth seeking rests on the authenticity of the truth seekers and on how ready and willing they are to give an account of their own intelligent operations. Facts clearly in our faces can be bent to suit our agendas. The thinker can cheat. The operator of the mind needs to be held accountable for his or her findings. The thinker, in science and in theology, needs to face up to bias. The human being needs to be an authentic soul-self. Such a self is the person capable of self-knowledge and accountability not only personally but communally and socially. Intentionality charting of one's interiority can be of service to provide credibility in this venture.

We have defined "soul" as the human psyche become conscious in the distinct operations of the human spirit. Charting of intentionality would have the operations of both named, known, and accounted for. We also suggest that the organism, in this case the brain, *mediates* the functions of the human spirit and the powerful energy of the psyche with its images. The brain mediates the operations of the operator, the human subject, as it communicates with the rest of reality. With interiority analysis we have a modest beginning account of what empirical functions belong properly to the human spirit, just as science has revealed the functions of the human organism and specifically of the brain.

The attempt we have made to redefine the soul and body in terms of the functions of organism, psyche, and spirit offers an empirical possibility to the sciences to ground religious experience. This grounding allows us to pose the question of how faith functions. The human spirit and its operations are natural and constitutive of the human being. The human is thus "spiritual" by nature. How then do grace and faith function in this humanness? What do they add? Because the human is naturally spiritual, even prior to any explicit religious identification, the operation of the human in its relatedness to the environment and cosmos is a spiritual issue. It may not be a religious issue for some. The philosophy of science can only point to the plausibility of the questions of an Ultimate Reality. If the question of God is unavoidable, the attempts to answer the question are clearly multiple. For example, the study of religion and its many forms is the study of how the spiritual human being expresses its relationship to Ultimate Reality. Such religious study need not presume a faith relationship with the Divine and thus is called "religious studies." The discipline that deals with Ultimate Reality as that reality that is related to the human in *faith* is theology.

For too long theology has been disconnected from cosmic moorings. This connection anchors the human and gives it a voice and choice for the ongoing shaping of matter in the universe. The human spirit as we have explained it is the seat of the intelligence and choice that will decide our future or, more radically, determine whether we will even have one. The operative functions of the human spirit—experiencing, understanding, judging, and choosing—provide the entry point for the influence of the Divine. But whether or not this divine influence is admitted, human operations, operating poorly or well, will determine the future of cultures. Can we afford the continued isolation of the human bent on being accountable to no one? What are the interdisciplinary links we need to shape an adequate study of spirituality?

The Relational Links

What is spirituality? Is it religion? Is it holiness? Does it have anything at all to do with science? These questions from the man and woman on the street press us to clarify terms we bandy about, often unsure of what we mean by them. It is clear from our approach to the soul as a natural component of the human, distinguished from the organism by certain operations, that we are referring to something radically human, not divine. True, the human person is *deified*[11] in the very substance of its operations as it comes more and more under the influence of the Divine. But it behooves us to understand what it is that will be transformed. Human relationship with the Divine describes *holiness* and the unfolding of how grace, virtue, and the gifts of the Spirit bring that holiness about. Spirituality is the real presence of the human, in its conscious operations, mediating that presence to the rest of reality. The intentional nurturing of the human spirit can be called "spiritual development" in contrast to "human development," of which it is a part, for human development would include the unfolding of the organism and the psychic/emotional life of the human person. *Christian* spirituality is that real presence directly influenced by the person and life of Jesus, the Christ. One has a spirituality by simply being human, no matter how deformed, reformed, or transformed that presence to the world may be. One has a spirituality and may or may not have a

[11] This term, originating in Eastern Orthodoxy, is used by Daniel Helminiak in a discussion of the theotic viewpoint held by believers (*Religion and the Human Sciences: An Approach via Spirituality* [New York: SUNY, 1998], 124ff.).

religion. A religion is an organized system marked by a distinct creed, code, and cult. The religion can be corrupt or healthy. The role of religion is to support and nourish human spirituality so that the human can make the choices needed to move the culture forward.

If spirituality is the way one is present in the world, then what is the relationship of spirituality to morality? Morality is the outer behavioral manifestation of one's spirituality. Morality is one piece with spirituality. Touch one, and you have touched the other. The beauty of human spirituality will be known by the moral choices one makes. The struggle to make morally responsible choices, the choices of an authentic human being, reveals the beauty of one's spirituality. Spirituality may manifest, or keep hidden and implicit, a deep faith relationship with the Divine. What one *sees* is often *not* what one gets.

A Blessed Accountability

What we have attempted here is an overview of reclaiming and redefining the human soul in a way that might be intelligible to the human and to the natural sciences. However, knowing is not enough. Consciousness presses toward the "so what," the *value* of rethinking what the human is—and more, what we as thinking humans intend to do about it. What difference does it make to know *how* I function as an organism/psyche/spirit?

The answer summons us to become an active partner in our own spiritual development. What we as human beings know and what we do about what we know matters. We are not an island. As we become more and more humanly authentic, the culture progresses. As we make choices influenced by bias, the culture declines. Nothing is left untouched, unchanged, or neutral. We are watching human culture change around us daily through the choices we and others make. We are poised in the humanity of our little lives to add our choices to the whole. In our science and in our theology, we stand accountable. In our homes, our parishes, our communities, our nations, our cultures, our universe, we will be measured. Such is our freedom. Such is our dignity. Out of these we shape the future. What might this shaping mean? If reclaiming our souls is the first step, how does the quality of our human authenticity transform culture?

Measuring the Culture

Culture is shaped by the meanings and values of human beings in a distinct environment. Contrary to the past, when the Christian European culture was presupposed as normative, today cultural anthropologists point out that a culture is shaped by human beings who intend meaning and who treasure distinct values that shape decision. Culture is spoken of today in the plural, the Western Christian European culture being one in the midst of cultures that are African, Indonesian, Korean, and Latino/a, to name but a few.

If culture is shaped by what human beings mean and value, then the culture, wherever it is found, can be measured by the quality of what people intend and the values people safeguard. If taking a life in your culture is murder and means you are to be executed, life for the people who practice such capital punishment is regarded basically as a physical reality with physical consequences. You take a life, you give yours. In such a culture, those for whom life means more than mere physical existence and who therefore oppose capital punishment are regarded as soft, pandering to criminals. It is the *meaning* accepted by those in power in the culture that will determine the practice. The culture would be transformed if the meaning of life as much more than physical were to be considered and intended. When human life is understood also as psychospiritual, capable of change, repentance, and forgiveness, its *meaning* has changed, and the value placed on human life, even that of the murderer, is heightened. When this meaning and value shift, so does the culture shift.

This understanding brings a proportion to our sense that "this is just the way it is." No, it isn't just the way it is. It is the way we *decide* it will be. The habit of smoking in America is one example. Twenty years ago the naysayers were loud in their claims that nothing would change our nicotine addiction in society. As the scientific data became clearer and clearer, the *meaning* and consequences of what smoking does to human health raised the consciousness of Americans significantly. As awareness grew, the *value* of smoking plunged. Now tobacco companies have been sued for influencing cigarette addiction through advertising. There is *value* today in the fact that people have been able to stop smoking. Laws have now been passed to prohibit smokers from infecting others in public places. The reversal is amazing. It is changing the culture.

A similar process is going on with the meaning of war and violence. The media has helped the peoples of the world come to terms with the truth of war. The result is a change in what war *means* today. Because its violence is no longer glorified, its *value* is suspect. War is fast becoming globally unacceptable for the resolution of conflict. In both these examples, cultures are changing as a result of these changes in meaning and value.

When a human being functions, whether in worship or in government, the operations of understanding and intent create meaning. That meaning will in turn influence what is valued. Religion has a powerful role in the culture that houses it. It influences what being human means. It is not only culture that must be measured. Religion in its deformed manifestations can betray the culture that hosts it. Waco, Jonestown, and Heaven's Gate are modern examples. So religion too must be ready to be accountable. Both must come before the bar of authentic human assessment in community. What are basic human rights? Who is entitled to them? The answers to these questions must be sought without bias as much as possible. Adequate answers will be given only from a sound critique of our present cultural practice and the support religion gives to those practices.

Thematizing how the human empirically arrives at meaning and value would give us the anthropological foundation for the transformation of culture. Religious inner transformation is referred to as "conversion," and conversion has everything to do with spirituality. Authentic human accountability empowered by genuine religion is in the business of soul making, and the quality of that soul will be the measure of the culture, for better or worse.

Summary

1. The term "soul" has become ambiguous and unclear in common usage. If the term is to be useful today, "soul" needs to be redefined *functionally* in terms of human operations and human consciousness.

2. The first axial shift is the global realization that individuals, through their ability to think, can exert reasonable control over natural forces and can be held responsible for their moral behavior. The second axial shift is the gradual, growing realization in our own time that no amount of control of natural forces assures human security without an accountability for the *operations of human consciousness* that culminate in human choices. This shift can be identified as an attentiveness to *philosophic interiority*.

3. Philosophic interiority is the thematic objectification of the operations of the human subject. Such objectification requires a careful attentiveness to one's own conscious operations. Identification of one's own operations is called "interiority analysis." It is done by the empirical observation of one's own intent, or *intentionality*.

4. The anthropology needed for interiority analysis is one that includes a charting of human consciousness. An adequate anthropology needs to be grounded in the *observation* of the operations of the human consciousness, as well as the *identification* and grouping of them according to similarity or *levels* (e.g., experiencing, understanding, judging, and deciding). Empirical identification of one's own operations is called "self-appropriation."

5. If the operations of human consciousness can be empirically observed through interiority analysis, and if an account of one's intent can be thematized, resulting in self-appropriation, then we, in the *decisions* made in this process, become responsible for the *progress or decline of cultures*. What has been neglected can be attended to, and what has been in excess can be altered. *Intent* in world affairs can no longer be ignored.

CHAPTER TWO

Spirituality as
a Universal Phenomenon

An Experience and a Study

In the introduction we spoke of spirituality as the distinct way the human is present in the world. It will be important to tease out what that might mean in greater detail, again clarifying how the terms "spirituality," "holiness," "religion," "human development," and "spiritual development" might differ and still be related.[1] Sandra Schneiders writes of spirituality as "the experience of conscious involvement in the project of life-integration through self-transcendence toward the ultimate value one perceives."[2] In giving this definition, Schneiders identifies spirituality as an *experience.* It is one thing to attempt to describe an experience. It is something else *to study* the phenomena of such experiences and point out how they effect change in human consciousness. The first focuses on spirituality as practiced, the second on spirituality as a discipline that studies the experience academically.

Based on the distinctions we have made about human interiority, I suggest that the experience Schneiders is defining above is really the intentional *development* of one's spirituality. In contrast, I have suggested that the human person is spiritual *before any intentionality begins.* The human person is spiritual by nature, even though that spirituality might remain truncated or undeveloped. This would mean that

---

[1] For a good clarification of some of these terms, see William G. Thompson, "Spirituality, Spiritual Development, and Holiness," *Review for Religious* 51:5 (September–October 1992): 646–56.

[2] "The Study of Christian Spirituality: Contours and Dynamics of a Discipline," *Christian Spirituality Bulletin* 6:1 (Spring 1998): 1 and 3.

the mentally impaired, the insane, and the unborn are spiritual beings simply because they are human. This clarification distinguishes spirituality from any particular religious framework while understanding spirituality to be central to any authentic religious system. For many, spirituality and religion are synonymous. What I am suggesting is that the human is spiritual by constitution whether the person is religious or not. The spiritual functions can be identified as conscious experience, questioning for understanding, reaching a judgment as a result of that questioning, and then weighing how valuable the stakes are in acting out of what we know to be true. These spirit functions identify us as spiritual beings. They are functions that exceed mere psychic or physical functioning. The "conscious involvement" Schneiders describes is, I believe, the human spirit setting about the process I would describe as "spiritual development."

Clarifying Development Terms

It remains for us to address other terms such as "human development," "spiritual development," and "holiness." *Human development* is the unfolding of the human person in its totality. It refers to physical development, psychic or emotional maturing, and the functioning of the intentional operations of the human spirit identified as intelligence and free choice. *Spiritual development* focuses on the distinctly spiritual functions of human development and the unfolding of the conscious human spirit, specifically those functions that have to do with one's capacity to wonder, know, and choose. *Holiness* is a distinctly religious term. It refers to the change in a human being as a result of a relationship with the Divine, however one conceptualizes that relationship.

Religion

Spiritual development becomes *religious* if the person draws from an organized religious tradition whose creed, code, and cult become a vital part of that spiritual development. Can a person develop *spiritually* while not belonging to any distinct religion? As we have defined spiritual growth, yes, someone could be deeply spiritual while identifying with no specific religion. Yet I will suggest that spiritual growth can be brought to its fullest maturity only with a communal dimension, being in relation to others, human and divine, in some form of embodied worship. A spirituality that avoids outer expression and relationship with others risks the danger of condemning itself to isolationism and abstraction.

To point out how these clear distinctions can be helpful in a practical way, a Down syndrome adult may be reverent and loving, due to careful upbringing and a real relationship with God, but not manifest the overall human development characteristic of an adult of his or her age. Spiritual development may include an explicit reference to the Holy or the transcendent in the person's life, or it may stay at a rather undeveloped level where the self, money, or power is supreme. If these are made the goal of one's conscious involvement, that involvement reveals a spirituality sorely limited to passing things, but the function and pursuit of them, no matter how limited, are still *spiritual* operations. They are undertaken with intelligence and choice, and these are distinct functions of the human *spirit*, even if the person uses the functions to deny the very existence of God.

Holiness

Holiness is a different matter. It is a cultivated and intentional pursuit of a *relationship with the mystery of the transcendent* in one's life. It reveals an ongoing transformation of the human spirit *in explicit relation to the Divine*. Holiness is distinct from religion, for some give lip service to a religious tradition while being quite self-preoccupied. In contrast, once a relationship with the Holy is established, religious expression becomes the outer manifestation of this inner reality. This means that religion, when authentic, has both an inner and an outer dimension.

What we have here is an attempt to clarify what can be quite murky and ambiguous in general spiritual writings. Spirituality pertains to the very nature of human beings. They function spiritually when they consciously know and choose. One's spirituality is religious if the person belongs to a religious tradition that nourishes one's spirituality. Holiness is the personal relationship one has with the Holy. This holiness is the heart of the matter. It is the soul of religious practice. Spiritual development is the unfolding of the operations of the distinctly human spirit, the self-reflective consciousness—namely, wonder, inquiry, reflection, and evaluation, leading to knowing and choosing. Spiritual development manifests functions that are distinctly human. Human development is the *total* development of the human, physically, psychically, and spiritually. Human development shares some common features with the animal world. For the believer, human development is not complete without spiritual development, and spiritual development is fed by the religious nourishment that results in real holiness.

This brings us back to what we have defined spirituality to be. At the risk of being simplistic, I'm going to affirm what I suggested earlier, that spirituality is being really present. It is *being all there*. It will take the rest of this book to explain what this means. For now it is enough to say that *spirituality is a real presence*. Truly spiritual human beings are in touch with themselves, learn more about themselves daily, agonize over their dreams and limits, and are at home in their skin. The human presence we are referring to is *real*; it grows daily in relationship with all else that is real. The result is a happy and beautiful human being. In common parlance we talk about *beautiful people*, folks who "have it all together." Much of the exploration ahead will deal with what it is that they have all together!

Today spirituality begs a definition from the roots up. The human being is either spiritual by its very creation or simply a complex arrangement dictated by DNA. If the human is distinctly spiritual, and religious traditions have always claimed so, we need the sciences to acknowledge this truth also. We need to give an account of how this is so in a way that is intelligible to the sciences, however tentative that account might be. We have been sketching out a framework for spirituality by clarifying our terms. It now remains for us to fill in the sketch.

Historical Sketch

Then and Now

Spirituality as an academic discipline is somewhat of a newcomer. It has not always held a rightful place in the academy.[3] Prior to the Second Vatican Council, spirituality referred to anything, any object, any action or person, perceived to be under the influence of God. Its reference was immediately to the Divine. It had to do with God entering the human sphere. It automatically implied holiness or something to do with the sacred. Very often spirituality referred to a charism, a blessing, a hymn, or a religious ritual, and this meaning remains alive today. This usage was an attempt to distinguish the *pneumaticos* from the *psychikos anthropos*, the Holy Spirit's activity in the human from

[3] For an excellent coverage of this development, see Sandra Schneiders, "Spirituality in the Academy," *Theological Studies* 50 (1989): 676–97.

the human's own activity. We might say this distinction was an effort to differentiate grace from nature, the action of God from purely human action. In differentiating, however, the human propensity to separate or oppose also tends to be automatic. What can be distinguished need not be separated. An example is our very lifeblood. We can *distinguish* red and white corpuscles and plasma, but if we have whole blood, they are not *separate*.

We know today, theologically, that there is no such thing as *pure nature*, that is, the existence of any creature on its own without reference to its Creator. All created reality exists only because of this reference. There is no such thing as nature without the creative presence of the Creator sustaining it in existence. Among nonbelievers, this faith position is an affront to autonomy, and the autonomous, nondependent human is the ideal.

Yet the Enlightenment has happened, the sciences have flourished, and the questions, old and new, beg answers. Does the distinction between human and divine activity, which we have already begun to pursue in this study, presume a *competition* between human and divine? In the recent past, spiritual dualism unfortunately would presume so, and it will be part of our purpose to show this competitive view to be false.

In Between

By 1600 this competitive assumption was so common that spirituality referred almost exclusively to one's *interior life*, meaning the life of the soul in its relationship to God. It was presumed that only those who had such an interior life had a spirituality, and spirituality was synonymous with religiosity.[4] By 1700 this was so much the case that a spiritual elitism prevailed: only those in monasteries or members of the clergy were presumed to be spiritual. That a lay Christian might be spiritual was the exception, and it was presumed that those of other faith traditions could not be saved, because they had no possibility of a spiritual life. Unfortunately, this is the mentality still found among some Christians of various denominations, although this point of view is quickly changing.

---

[4] Much of the history barely sketched here is summarized well in Walter Principe, "Toward Defining Spirituality," *Studies in Religion / Sciences Religieuses* 12:2 (June 1983): 127–41.

New Wine

The second axial shift, the shift to philosophical interiority, has brought spirituality to the forefront. The new interest has caused a scramble to clarify what is meant by the vocabulary we use. It is anyone's guess as to what spirituality really is. We cannot go back to the old dualistic wineskins, because they are no longer accurate or adequate, so we are pressed to examine this dimension of human life anew. It becomes critical to clarify terms. In discussing spirituality, we are no longer necessarily discussing one's religious affiliation, yet we will not exclude it. We are not referring merely to developmental stages of human growth, but we don't want to exclude them either. We are not referring only to one's personal relationship with the Divine, yet we know this figures in the equation somewhere. As spirituality seriously enters the academy, theology, with its call to clearly define what we mean, might help to clear up the ambiguity.

Spirituality and Theology

A Troubled Marriage

The relationship between spirituality and theology can be likened to a troubled marriage.[5] In the early patristic period, theology was still rooted in the *spiritual experience* flowing from contact with the scriptural word. Theology was reflection on one's *experience* of God. We might say the two are indeed in one flesh, the marriage firmly established.

Divorce

By the Middle Ages an estrangement develops, leading to separation and divorce. Philosophy begins to supplant Scripture in supplying the categories for the pursuit of systematic theology. Thomas puts spirituality in part II of the *Summa Theologiae* as a subdivision of moral theology. Instead of being the very fountainhead of theological reflection as it had been earlier, spirituality becomes a mere subdivision of moral theology, and the term "spiritual theology" begins to be used

[5] Much of the content for this discussion I owe to Sandra Schneiders's careful work in the writings referred to earlier and also in her article "Theology and Spirituality: Strangers, Rivals, or Partners?," which first appeared in *Horizons* 13:2 (1986): 253–74.

to refer to it, as if there could be another kind. Subtly implied here is that theology now is "on its own" academically, not to be confused with religious experience. This experience belongs to the monastery or retreat house and is designated as the "interior life." Because of its subjectivity, it is not to intrude on the academy. Spiritual experience refuses to be rationally controlled and may even defy rational classification due to its mysterious, mystical nature.

By 1600–1800 the wedge between spirituality and theology is formalized. The use of interior-life terminology for spirituality prevails, and the elite class system dividing "religious" folk from the "laity" is firmly in place. Spiritual theology is now divided into *ascetical* and *mystical* theology, studied under morality. In keeping with a growing elitism, ascetical theology is presumed to pertain to the ordinary Christian, while mystical theology attempts to explain the interior lives of priests and those in religious lifestyles. The class system in place is based on unquestioned assumptions about spirituality.

This unfortunate divorce overlooked the fact that many ordinary Christians were living lives of extraordinary heroism, lives of profound prayer and spiritual development. These facts were concrete contradictions to the formal divisions referred to in writings on spirituality. Ordinary Christians were thought to have no access to the techniques necessary for an advanced interior life. These were to be found among religious and clerics. And so the conclusion was falsely reached that ordinary Christians couldn't possibly have a deep spirituality.

Reconciliation and Renewal

This state of affairs lasted into the twentieth century. With Vatican II (1962–65) the system began to crumble. In its first document on the church, *Lumen Gentium*, the council sounded the *universal call to holiness*. The words rang out like a trumpet blast that shattered the artificial mental constructs that had prevailed for centuries. In its second document on the church, the much less read *Gaudium et Spes*, the council offered a view of the church in the world that to this day is not fully understood or taken seriously even by Catholic Christians. These documents place the church *in the midst of the world* as light, joy, and hope for the nations. This new perspective jolted not only the church but the whole human family with the shocking assertion that every man, woman, and child on the face of the earth is called to holiness. The universal call to holiness presented theology with the challenge to explain how this could be so when so many of those called to holiness would never feel the waters of baptism, much less have access to religious practices reserved in the past to an elite.

The response was immediate. Theologians quickly moved to explore religious experience as a universal phenomenon, and the term "spirituality" began to replace the term "spiritual theology" with its two-part division. The discipline of spirituality began to be restored in its own right, and the wedge between religious experience and theology gradually began to narrow. Spirituality as a discipline has become the study of religious experience, and it is clear that this experience is happening all over the world in every religious tradition. Christian theology welcomes the study of spirituality as a discipline in its midst, clarifying what a distinctly Christian spirituality is in the midst of the richness found in other traditions. The original patristic insight is restored—that spirituality is the fountainhead of theological reflection—but with a contemporary modification: materialistic secularism. Our time needs to deal seriously with the secular rejection of religious faith and institutionalized religion. Explicit *religious* meaning in spiritual experience can no longer be assumed. Those who have not been privy to faith communities are having religious experiences but do not even know how to word what they are experiencing. In fact, some are inventing cults and sects to provide a home for what they have experienced because up to now they have been religiously homeless.

Systematic theology has scrambled to develop categories for different types of religious experience. With the entry of the psychological sciences, emphasis has shifted from *what* is apprehended in such experience to *how* it is apprehended. No longer are science and psychology merely "secular" subjects. They have become interdisciplinary partners in the study of spirituality. New questions emerge. Is the human being in some way "wired" for religious experience? Answers and clarifications are sought in an interdisciplinary way from theology, psychology, and science. Once the distortions of previous centuries are identified and put aside, it becomes clear that the human being is spiritual by its very nature. Religious and mystical experience are no longer dismissed as nonscientific, nonempirical, and purely subjective. Such experience is common. It is now studied in relation to comparative religion, anthropology, history, literary interpretation, and the theory of myth and symbol in various cultures.

I have suggested that as a global phenomenon, spirituality is the distinct presence a human being brings to one's culture and religious tradition. The first quality of this presence is a type of *openness*. Perhaps a better way to name what I mean by this would be to use the word "wonder." I propose that the capacity for wonder is evidence of the innate spirituality of the human being. Because of this quality of wonder, spirituality is always *implicitly religious, even if its* religious dimension is *explicitly denied*. Spirituality becomes explicitly religious when it is expressed and nourished through a distinct religious symbol system. Religion has an inner core and an outer manifestation.[6] The inner core has to do with the direct action of the Spirit of God in the human heart. The outer manifestation will take the shape of a particular tradition with its various rituals, beliefs, and symbols. This allows us to make the following respectful distinctions:

- *Christian spirituality* is authentic human presence to lived reality in light of the explicit mystery of Christ Jesus.

- *Jewish spirituality* is authentic human presence to lived reality in light of the explicit centrality of the Torah.

- *Islamic spirituality* is authentic human presence to lived reality in light of the explicit centrality of the teachings of Muhammad in the Qur'an.

- *Hindu spirituality* is authentic human presence to lived reality in light of the explicit belief in release from karmic rebirth.

- *Buddhist spirituality* is authentic human presence to lived reality in light of the explicit belief in the release from human desire that leads to suffering.

- *Primal spirituality* is authentic human presence to lived reality in light of the explicit centrality of the Holy mysteriously present in nature.

With this variety before us, how is spirituality to be studied? Its history can be explored in a more expansive way than this brief sketch has provided. But more importantly, the study of spirituality needs a *methodology*, one that is anthropologically grounded. Other disciplines, the sciences in particular, need an *empirical* entry point into conversation about the spiritual dimension of the human person.

---

[6] Bernard Lonergan uses this expression in *Method in Theology* in his chapter on "Foundations" (London: Darton, Longman and Todd, 1972), 284. He states clearly that only the inner core is transcultural.

Spirituality as a Discipline

As a field of study, spirituality attempts to investigate spiritual experience in an interdisciplinary way. It seeks to explain this experience as such, that is, as spiritual and as experience. As it is pursued today, the study of spirituality draws from the religious tradition that grounds it if this is explicit, and it draws from the human and natural sciences. If the religious tradition of the person involved makes use of a theological framework for reflection, the theology will be studied. If not, more philosophical questions regarding the human person might be asked. As might be expected, prime conversationalists in this interdisciplinary approach will be the psychological sciences. The social sciences might also be pursued to shed light on the cultural dimensions of experience. Finally, the findings of the natural sciences in anthropology, biology, and physics will play a key part. Careful work done on the human elements of this experience allows for clear distinctions between the *human* functioning under study and the *divine* activity always presumed present among believers. If we are to avoid the old dualism, the key question becomes "What is the precise *relationship* between this human and the Divine?" This question reopens the discussion of the nature-grace relationship in a new and exciting way.

The study of spirituality will also need to be descriptive/critical rather than prescriptive/normative. In the past, one form of spiritual experience was considered the norm, and all other experiences were evaluated in light of the experience considered normative. If the experience fell short, it would be judged deficient, and suggestions would be prescribed to make it "measure up." Today, in contrast, varieties of spiritual experience are approached with reverence, and the student asks those involved to explain it on its own terms. The student will then add this explanation to those already gathered, and all will be scrutinized. The critical aspect will be sound if the person doing the critique has some understanding of interiority and is able to do some intentionality analysis. A clear understanding of how consciousness functions will give the student an anthropological framework for grounding religious experience in human consciousness. Clear description and questioning can lead to a tentative explanation. An insight Lonergan adds here is the importance of clarifying the point of view of the student doing the study. The student has a point of view, and if it is not acknowledged and declared honestly, the student's assumptions will be operative anyway, and this perspective may act as a bias, admitting only elements of the experience that correspond to his or her own position.

The study of spirituality needs to be ecumenical, interreligious, and cross-cultural. A person doing studies in spirituality today cannot be of the mind that one's faith tradition is the only one that holds truth and the authentic activity of the Divine. Rather, an attitude of awe and watchfulness is assumed, lest one miss the truth or activity experienced by another. As wisely observed by scholars in this field, the person doing this theological work must be totally committed to his or her faith tradition. One who is superficially committed will vacillate left and right to please the dialogue partners, seeking to be neutral. This offers no service to those seeking to understand clear differences. What is needed is a deeply committed scholar who is open to what he or she might learn from others—such a person is a rarity and a gift!

Finally, the study of spirituality today needs to be holistic and inclusive of both the explicitly *religious* aspect of human experience and the more explicitly *secular* aspect. The distorted notions of the past, that spirituality belonged somehow only to a spiritual elite, must give way to a critical observation of what is happening to a large majority of human beings in every walk of life. The study, as it progresses, is gradually revealing the unity of experience in its sacred and secular dimensions rather than the separation into two separate "worlds" of what has been labeled as the "sacred" and the "secular." As Islam puts it, the Holy is closer than one's jugular vein.

This breaking down of the strict *separation* of sacred and secular while clarifying their *differences* presents the challenge of explaining how each is *distinct* while *interrelated*.

The Method Used in This Study

As indicated in the introduction, what is needed for the pursuit of the study of spirituality is attentiveness to the human person in a way often neglected in the past. Because the study is interdisciplinary, the operations of the human subject must become the object of careful and critical observation. Intentionality analysis will be used. One's own consciousness will be the primary referent. A key question will be "How does the activity of the Divine upon the human manifest itself in consciousness?" Can this activity be empirically verified?

There are academic steps in the study of spirituality, just as there are academic steps in theological study. The spiritual experience studied must be *researched,* and the data uncovered must be attended to. This particular study will limit itself to spiritual experience that is both

Christian and religious. What is discovered in this tradition needs to be *interpreted* in terms of that tradition and its place among other religious traditions. The data uncovered needs to be *historically* clarified. What data has been moving forward in the tradition and its place in the wider world? Varied interpretations need to be evaluated in terms of *dialectical* worth or effectiveness. Does the experience enhance the human? How so? Does it contribute positively to culture? In other words, how does one evaluate its *fruit*? Does the spiritual or religious experience manifest *foundational* conversion or a transformation of life? Finally, how do we formulate an accurate *doctrine* regarding spirituality, interconnect those doctrines *systematically*, and then *communicate* them effectively to others? In summary, the methodological steps are *research, interpretation, history, dialectic, foundations, doctrines, systematics,* and *communication*.

The positive values that are constitutive of authentic Catholic religious spiritual experience will without doubt come to bear on this study. Catholicity in its deeper meaning as an openness to the truth in its fullness wherever found will be pursued in contrast to a more sectarian interpretation of catholicity. In its deeper meaning, catholicity is not the private property of one community of faith. Rather, as proclaimed in the creeds recited Sunday after Sunday in various denominations, catholicity is the mark of the authentic truth seeker wherever he or she is to be found. It is in this broader sense that the term will be used, without neglecting its use to identify those who have been baptized into the institutional reality of the Catholic community. We now need to turn our focus to what is distinctive of Christian spirituality as it takes its place in the midst of the religious traditions of the world.

Summary

1. The clarification of the meaning of the terms used in the study of spirituality is of prime importance to avoid ambiguity. "Spirituality" refers to the total presence of a person to his or her milieu. It includes human development (of which spiritual development is but a part), holiness or the lack of it, and religion or its absence. "Human development" is the unfolding of the physical, psychic, and spiritual dimensions of the human being. "Spiritual development" involves the transformation of the human spirit, the capacity to wonder, question, reflect, and evaluate with a view to making a decision. It includes the

possibility of "holiness," or the intimate relationship one might have with the Divine. It is influenced by the presence or absence of "religion," a recognized set of beliefs, conduct, and rituals flowing from a core religious experience.

2. The history of spirituality reveals a movement in understanding from exclusive elitism to a universal call to every human being. The present time recognizes spirituality as constitutive of humanness. It understands Christian theology as the discipline that reflects and articulates spiritual experience through a distinct christological, sacramental, and communal lens.

3. Theology's relationship to spirituality reflects the history of spirituality. From a mere subdivision of normative moral theology to the universal reality that Christian theology in its various fields now serves, spirituality is taking its place as the meeting place for both theology and science. The key to the success of this meeting is interiority: understanding the dynamic operations of human consciousness.

CHAPTER THREE

The Distinctness
of Christian Spirituality

As Christians we are becoming more and more aware of ourselves as citizens of the world and as having a distinct religious tradition that is not like those of our neighbors. In a ghetto mentality one does not have to worry about "the others." But as a citizen of the world the Christian rubs shoulders with Jews, Muslims, Baha'i, Buddhists, Taoists, Jains, Sikhs, and tribal peoples. In today's world, Christians number approximately 2.2 billion. The Jewish community numbers approximately 18 million worldwide, and the Islamic community 1.6 billion.[1] In the United States, Catholics number 57 million, Protestants number 112 million, and Orthodox Christians number 0.8 million. The Jewish community in the United States numbers about 2.7 million, and the Islamic community numbers about 1.3 million.[2] The pluralism is evident and the diversity grows each day. People of diverse traditions live next door, work beside us, and search for the Divine in their lives as do we.

This reality challenges the Christian to assume a new posture in the culture. In the past we often retreated into our respective ghettos and snubbed the other as "not one of us." Today we are encouraged to welcome the other, dialogue with other traditions, and listen to one another as we try to explain our religious experience and our beliefs. It is in the midst of difference that one really comes to know oneself, and this present-day communal challenge is no exception. It is in attempting

---

[1] *Wikipedia*, s.v. "Major Religious Groups," last modified August 5, 2012, http://en.wikipedia.org/wiki/Major_religious_groups.

[2] Unites States Census Bureau, "The 2012 Statistical Abstract," sec. 1, p. 61, http://www.census.gov/compendia/statab/2012edition.html.

to explain ourselves that we discover how contextually conditioned our language is and how incomprehensible that religious language can be to others seeking to understand us.

It is even more urgent today to clarify who we are and what we believe *for our own sakes*. All religious traditions are not the same, and those who simplistically bunch them together render no service. The challenge today is to speak of oneself with conviction in such a way as not to disparage others. Each tradition is convinced its way is best. If we were not convinced that Christianity was the best way to live a human life religiously, why would we remain Christian? Is it possible to hold one's position firmly and still listen respectfully to others? I suggest that it is actually firm conviction and commitment that frees me to do so.

I have described spirituality as real or authentic human presence in the world. It is now time to try to sketch the distinct *kind* of presence the Christian brings to the world community. What I sketch here is not the private property of Christians but rather the emphasis that Christians offer to the human family. I propose that the Christian brings

1. a *communal/relational* presence, when others may prefer a more isolationist or individualist way of being in the world;

2. an *incarnational/integrative* approach to life in contrast to one more suspicious of matter, emotion, sexuality, the body, and the senses;

3. a *sacramental/liturgical* presence to the world community, when others may prefer to distance themselves from incorporating the mundane and material in religious ritual and celebration.

Each of these characteristics takes its cue from the heart of Christian religious experience: the incarnation of the Divine in human flesh in the person of Christ Jesus. Christians believe that the very self-expression of God is found in the Jewish Jesus of Nazareth, that God has chosen to "speak human" as a way to reveal both the Divine and the human to us in the relationship they share.

A Communal/Relational Presence

The Jewish Jesus was part of a people. That people believed that salvation came to those who stayed a part of the *qa'hal*, or community, and that salvation was in doubt for those who separated themselves from this association. Drawing from this social and religious experience, Jesus gathered a band around himself. He ate, slept, and traveled with this band. As he is depicted in the gospels, Jesus is rarely alone, and when he is, that solitude has a reference to others. An undercurrent to all the gospel accounts is the fact that the incarnate Word in the human Jesus is intensely relational and that this same relationality is fostered in his followers. How might we identify it? I'm going to venture to call it a "we-consciousness" in contrast to a "me-consciousness." What identifies a person as communal is the relational way his or her consciousness works. The self-awareness of a person does not stop with oneself but identifies itself in connection or relationship with others. Try to dance the rhumba or play partners in Canasta without a we-consciousness. The opposite of this type of presence is almost easier to grasp. My friend has lost her husband. She comes home in the evening and cooks herself a bit of supper. It is very different for her to do this simple act now in contrast with cooking a simple supper when her husband was present to share it with her. Me-consciousness can become ingrown. We are repelled by the self-centered behavior of the young teen who has no remorse in hitting a child while speeding around the neighborhood. The narcissism of such a self-awareness strikes us as selfish and immature.

The Christian believes firmly that faith in Christ Jesus sealed in public baptism makes one a "member of the church." A more relational rather than juridical way of saying it would be to say that the baptismal commitment makes one a disciple, a follower, of Jesus. The follower tries to "put on the mind" of the master. Coming directly from our Semitic roots in Jesus, Christian communities evidence a communal sense, ranging from the expediency of Congregationalist congregations, who leave gathering quite optional, to Catholic parishes that identify members "in good standing" as those who gather around the eucharistic table each Sunday. The communal/relational identity varies, but it is there, buffeted as it is in the United States by the winds of rugged individualism. If I identify myself as Christian, the next question usually is "What church?" and if Catholic, "What parish?" This is not the way the questioning might go with a Hindu or Buddhist acquaintance.

Jewish and Islamic communities share this we-consciousness with us but with marked differences. The basis for the relational and communitarian identity of the Christian is a belief that in the risen Christ *we are somehow joined to him and with one another*. This distinct tone to the sense of Christian community rests upon the identification of the group *as part of Christ's body*. It is understood that Jesus is risen and lives human life in a new way. By our baptism we are "in Christ Jesus" and share the beginnings of that new way of being human. We are on our way to this new kind of life. The identity of the group is not merely communal, as are others, but relational directly to Christ in one another. Christians who realize this truth believe that whatever they do to another human being they do to Christ. The bond or "glue" in this relationship is the Spirit of Jesus, the Holy Spirit. Like some living temple, built of living stones, the members of the Christian community are joined together in this Spirit. Together, ever being cleansed of sin and made holy, they move forward until the total cosmic Christ, head and members, "returns." No other religious tradition understands its "togetherness" in just this way. Christians—Catholic, Orthodox, and Protestant—with variations on the theme, own this vision in some form.

Finally, we need to ask where this conviction is rooted, and this query takes us back to the Christian doctrine of God. Basing its understanding on what Jesus revealed, the Christian community understands God as one, yet "doubly processing."[3] God as triune is revealed by Jesus. Without him, this knowledge about the "threeness" of God would be unknown to us. This is no small contribution to the religions of the world. What the revelation of Christianity offers is the one God self-expressing and self-offering. The one God is a deep and hidden Mystery. But God chooses not to remain hidden. The self-expression of God is complete and total. It is a Word—a "Son," relationally speaking—drawn from God's own spiritual divine substance, God's own birthing-mind, as it were.[4] Yet God is not only a dynamic birthing-Word-expression but also a loving self-gift of the Word. The Holy Spirit as God is an active, self-giving love. The gift of the Spirit then, births the Word in love *in us.* The procession of the Word and the spiration of the Spirit reveal a communal interdependence in God flowing out of *fullness*, not need. This mystery at the heart of Christianity is the wellspring of Jesus' own sense of *communio* as incarnate Word. Christians are thus joined together "in the name of the Father, the Son, and the Holy Spirit."

---

[3] This expression came to my attention for the first time in the systematic notes of professors in the 1980s at Regis College in Toronto.

[4] The term "Son" is not understood here as a biological generation. Christians do not believe that God has a biological son. The person of the Son is God's full, divine self-expression, thus equal to God's divine self, as is the self-giving love that is the Spirit.

An Incarnational/Integrative Presence

What does it mean to be saved? From what? By whom? For what? It is startling news to some Christians to realize that their notion of salvation may not be that of others.[5] Several religions consider salvation as a type of release from the limitations imposed by matter and embodiment. Some view the goal of human life as making choices that entitle one to join the ancestors as guardians of those still in this life. Yet others understand salvation as a type of ethical transformation of the human for the building up of the world.

The Christian enters this company with the startling point of view that salvation means *union with the Divine in love.* Where do Christians get this conviction? The Christian perspective comes from an experience, a religious experience in history. Christians believe that in the historical Jesus, a Jew, humankind was shown that salvation consists in the human indissolubly united to the Divine—in other words, that Jesus' own reality reveals what human salvation is. What is this reality that distinguishes the Christian understanding of what being saved means?

The doctrine of the incarnation states that Jesus is fully human and fully divine. Neither nature (the divine or the human consciousness) is compromised or violated in this union, called "hypostatic." There is only one person (subject) as a result of this union. The human consciousness of Jesus will function in his human organism/psyche/spirit as we have described earlier, and the eternal Word of God would respect that functioning. The fact that human nature is functioning takes nothing from the Divine that has bonded itself to it. On the contrary, such full and sinless functioning glorifies the Divine by letting it radiate *from and through that humanness.* What is human in Jesus is fully human. And what is divine in Jesus is fully divine. What is human is fully assumed by the Divine, yet there is no mixture. Christians believe this respectful union of the human and the Divine, more profound than a marriage, is revealed to the human community as the destiny for all humankind, for all peoples.

The implications of this incarnational reality on the way matter, the cosmos, nature, and the human itself are regarded are immense. Like the contact of some Midas touch, nothing can ever be the same.

---

[5] An excellent treatment of this realization is S. Mark Heim's *Salvations: Truth and Difference in Religion* (Maryknoll, NY: Orbis, 1995).

Because humanness was assumed in this union, DNA was assumed. The periodic table was assumed. Matter, like the humble scullery maid Cinderella, is transformed in the arms of the prince. All of matter becomes iconic of the Divine. Central to this revelation is the reclaiming of all that is genuinely human. It can't be stressed enough that authentic Christianity is based primarily on the *relationship* of that humanness to the Divine. The relationship is one of intimacy and friendship, not slavery and debasement. This is *good news*, a far cry from the terror regarding the Divine recorded in the history and archeology of various cultures. It is a far cry also from the distorted forms and practices Christianity itself has assumed in history. This union has everything to do with human trafficking, with pedophilia, with racism and sexism, for to abuse the human is to offer an affront to God. Something new is here. The newness proclaims the human as the very seat of the Holy. With that affirmation, every atom becomes a window into a dimension of reality that escapes the senses. Religions attempt to stutter some intelligible word about this reality. The spiritual pilgrim does well to associate with a tried-and-true wisdom community of fellow pilgrims who live out this vision. Christians need to find a way to express this vision of the human to those in other traditions. Everyone indeed has a word to offer, but only God has the *last* Word, one that is surprising. If we want to "see" God in this life, it points us to the mirror.

Many Christians have not come to terms with this simple but profound revelation. To do so would mean a profound change of perspective toward others. Christian responses have varied from a full, joyful realization found in the mystics to the hesitant caution found in Puritan reserve or fundamentalist rigidity. The fact remains. The central belief of the Christian tradition is that the Divine has united God's self to humanness to make clear God's intent for us. This God, a triunity, has come in language all can understand—human—to work out a communal salvation with us for everyone. This is Christian salvation. It is dynamic and ongoing, not once-and-for-all magic. It calls for the full operation of the human being—not as the *primary* cause of such salvation but as an *instrument*, a responder in a partnership project.

There are other lenses. There is the *pantheist* lens that claims all as divine, with no distinction between created and Creator. There is the *panentheist* lens that holds that the Divine is *in* everything somehow. There is the *theist* lens that accepts the Divine as real. There is the *nontheist* lens that holds that the Divine is not knowable and the *atheist* perspective that the Divine (at least as presented) does not exist.

There is the *deist* view that the Divine is unconcerned and the *fideist* view that belief in the Divine substitutes for human intelligence. None of these quite matches the focus of the authentic Christian lens.

If the Christian is to be known by an incarnational/integrative presence in the world, then the implications of this startling revelation are not minor. A spirituality so identified will need to address embodiment, not ignore it. It will need to understand its connection and relationship to the earth and its care, not look the other way when the earth is polluted and ravaged. It will understand itself as its brother's keeper, no matter what culture that brother or sister hails from. It will be present politically, economically, scientifically, artistically, and religiously to the world as a light shines forth from a lantern. A spirituality that is incarnational will be grounded. It will *really be present* to the world, be in the world, and thus be a vital part of transformative progress in whatever culture it finds itself.

A Sacramental/Liturgical Presence

The words "sacramental" and "liturgical" have a distinctly Catholic tone. I offer them here with a more nondenominational catholic meaning. I propose that the spirituality we have identified as distinctly Christian will demand a *sacramental* or sacred handling of all material reality as potentially revelatory of God's activity and presence. I also propose that the incarnational aspect of Christian spirituality will draw Christians to ground their religious experience in public and communal worship of some kind. This is what I mean by *sacramental* and *liturgical*. Created reality is intentionally included in the community's official worship celebrations. To be realistic, this public ritual form of worship can be messy. We have to deal with the concrete situations of real people. We like this; they like that. Public worship is a forum for making community real.

To understand what "sacramental" might mean in this broader sense, we need to return to the original experience of the Christian community, the experience of Jesus' sacred humanity. The human Jesus, as he was experienced by his early followers, was an inclusive *welcomer*. He sat at table with those considered outcasts. He conversed with publicans and sinners. This Jesus was a *strengthener*. He repeatedly told his followers not to be afraid, and he promised his Spirit to them after the trauma of his death and the shocking marvel of his resurrection. He was a *nurturer*. He nourished the hearts of those who listened to him with his teaching, and at times he provided for them physically. He was a *forgiver*. He called his followers to forgive not seven times but seventy times seven, making forgiveness a permanent Christian *posture* in the world. He was a *healer*. The sick of all kinds found restoration in him. He was a *leader*, not by the coercive power common among those in authority, but with the relational power that draws willing response from others. Finally, he was a genuine self-giving *lover*, one who gave of himself to those he loved without counting the cost. In these concrete instances, Jesus in his humanity is the *primary* sacrament. *His humanness mediates the Divine.* His sacred humanity is the bridge reaching out to meet us in our humanness and connecting us to the divine Mystery found in him.

In its magnificent obsession with this Word-in-our-flesh, the Christian community is not merely remembering a dead hero. The community believes he lives and is in our midst through the power of the Spirit. He is the head, and this ragtag community of sinner/saints is his body. The community longs to do what he did. It longs to inclusively *welcome* others. It longs to *strengthen* them and support them in the human struggle. It wants to *nourish* them, *forgive* them, and bring *healing* to them. It wants to *lead* in the way he did, relationally, by washing feet, and it wants to learn to *love* his way, beyond the self-seeking it can settle for when it forgets him. The community we call "church" is thus the *secondary* sacrament. Through its humanity, joined to Christ in grace, God mediates the Divine to the world. The fact that the community often fails at it, or does it poorly, does not change the reality of its mission. The Christian community is sacramental by its very nature. This Catholic sense would propose that the Christ is continually revealed in *both* Word and sacrament in the Christian community. What we are referring to here is called "sacramentality" in a substantive sense. It is this *substance* that is then celebrated *ritually* in worship. Without substantive grounding in the risen Christ, the ritual sacraments are in danger of collapsing into empty ritualism, a danger that has plagued the Christian community at different times in its history.

Only after these two senses of sacramentality are understood—a primary sacramentality in Jesus himself and a secondary sacramentality in his body, the church—can we properly understand the *ritual* sacraments that are celebrated in worship. In the Catholic, Orthodox, Lutheran, and Episcopal traditions, we find distinct *rituals* to celebrate the continuing activity of the risen Christ in the midst of the community. His inclusive welcoming is celebrated in the ritual of baptism, his strengthening in confirmation, his nourishing in the Eucharist, his forgiveness in reconciliation, his healing in the anointing of the sick, his leadership in orders, and his self-giving love in the ritual of marriage called matrimony. The fact that each Christian community does not have these *rituals* does not mean that the risen Christ is not active in the lives of its people. This activity is simply more hidden, not formally ritualized. Christians are sacramental because Jesus is the primary sacrament, and they are his followers doing the "Jesus thing." They are sacramental because their communities manifest the substantial activity of the risen Jesus alive and active in their midst. They are sacramental *ritually* when their official public worship rituals reveal and celebrate the risen Jesus active in their midst as they gather publicly together.

Likewise, the term "liturgical" can be understood substantially or ritually or both. The term most accurately refers to the official public religious worship of a group of Christians. Implied in the term is the understanding that the ceremony celebrates the action of the risen Christ in the midst of his people. Christian communities vary greatly in their liturgical expression. Some celebrate only the Word in public worship. Some celebrate both Word and sacrament at set times. Some celebrate sacramentally and liturgically weekly or daily.

What contrasts with this sacramental/liturgical presence in the world? One contrast would be a spirituality that seeks to be totally private and interior, one that has no public face, no sense of connection with day-to-day human struggle—a spirituality of the alone with the Alone. Another example might be the magical and manipulative approach to material things found in the occult. The goal is not a revealing of the Divine but some kind of mysterious control of a crystal, a pendulum, tarot cards, or a séance by a hidden power. Many walk these alternate paths. But it is the combination of the communal/relational, the incarnational/integrative, and the sacramental/liturgical expression that gives a distinct identity to those believers whose name is Christian.

The identity described above will bring a distinct presence, a distinct spirituality, to the world. To a greater or lesser degree, and often unwittingly, the Christian will bring this identity to his or her coworkers, neighbors, and friends. In return, the Christian will experience the spirituality of the Jewish community, the Islamic community, the Buddhist, Hindu, or Taoist community. Theirs too is a distinct kind of presence. In the foundations that follow, this distinct Christian identity will always be kept in view, and from the facts of that honesty, not arrogance, the interaction of the human and the Divine will be explored.

Summary

1. The Christian lives in a global human community. Persons in that world community have different spiritualities that ground a diversity of religious traditions. These spiritualities are not all the same, nor are the religious traditions that flow from them.

2. The Christian in today's global village is faced with the double challenge of a committed conviction of the truth of Christian revelation while being sensitively respectful of the lenses of others. It is possible to be respectful of another's lens while knowing it is not an adequate religious lens for oneself.

3. A spirituality that is to be identified as authentically Christian will have clear characteristics. Three such indicators of a distinctive Christian spirituality are that it is

- communal/relational,
- incarnational/integrative, and
- sacramental/liturgical.

Central to Christian identity is the mystery of the incarnation of God's Word in human form. From this central relational mystery flow the communal and sacramental aspects.

4. A clear understanding of this central mystery, the relationship of the Divine with the human, is central to the Christian's presence in the world, morally, socially, economically, culturally, politically, and religiously.

CHAPTER FOUR

The Anthropological Foundation

What framework for the human person will we use to ask how grace relates to the human person? The human side of the equation will deal with anthropology. What is this human being—how does it feel, think, choose? What is this constant longing for something more than itself? The divine side of the equation is the action of God upon the human being—grace, God's gift of God's very self to humans. What is the divine interaction with human functioning, and most importantly, how will we attempt to explain the Divine *relating* to the human in the ongoing conversion and the ongoing transformation of the human into a remarkably beautiful being?

With the incarnation as our pattern and keeping before us the remarkable courtesy extended to the human in its union with the divine Word in Jesus, we need to attend to how we regard the human and whether our understanding of it is adequate. Earlier in this study we stated that the usual *body, mind, and spirit* description used in pop culture is wanting. I offered instead the *organism, psyche, and spirit* dimensions as more anthropologically inclusive and workable. This suggestion is not new. It has been used in the writings of Daniel Helminiak and in the work of Robert Doran. What may be somewhat novel is my suggestion that the concept of "soul" be rethought in light of this framework.

The Human Organism

Organism, psyche, and spirit offer what might be called a "triple composite." That there are three *parts* to the human being is not what is meant by this triple-composite language. The human being is not like a three-storied house. The human being is a unified whole. The organism/psyche/spirit language I am suggesting refers to *dimensions* of the unified human being. The human spirit functions in its operations under the influence of psychic energy rooted in a living organism recognizable as human by a distinct DNA, and it refers to a biological physicality visible to the human senses. The diagrams on pages 113–15 will attempt to picture an active dynamism; thus, they will be faulty from the start because they are static images. What they refer to is not really the way it is. It is merely the way the diagram pictures it. But if we keep this limitation in mind, the diagrams may be useful.

It will also be good to keep in mind that the dimension of the human really most available to the natural sciences at this time in history is the organism. The human science of psychology continues to explore the psyche, and the human spirit for many remains a nebulous something that distinguishes the human from the animal and allows the human to have contact with the Divine. Some are tempted to simply identify the human spirit with the psyche. This could mean settling for a notion of spirituality collapsed into psychologism. We will carefully avoid this pitfall even as we honor the functions of each dimension and attempt to distinguish them.

The human can be viewed through various lenses. Daniel Helminiak suggests four anthropological viewpoints: positivist, philosophic, theist, and theotic. A viewpoint determines the perspective of the thinking subject. The *theotic viewpoint* holds that being is granted to the human creature by Another, the One who is. By the action of parents, a new life emerges at birth, hopefully with an organism equipped with all that pertains to the human species. Psychic energy, already sensitively active in the womb, orchestrates the slow process of cell development. As the activating *form* of the human matter provided by the ovum and sperm, the psychic energy also unfolds the sensitive and intelligent operations that are distinct to human functioning. The human spirit with its distinct operations of inquiry and choice waits for sufficient human development to ground its spiritual unfolding. But the potential for the development of the human spirit is there from the start and, unless thwarted, will unfold.

The Divine at this point, in the perspective of the believer, is the ground of that psychic energy or form. The divine Mystery is the source of the life of this creature. From this Life it receives life. The relationship at this point is merely that of origin. Meager as this may seem, it is the creative source of any further relationship that will develop. We might say the Divine at this early stage is like a hopeful beggar waiting in the wings to be recognized. The human consciousness, the unique and distinct manifestation of the human spirit, is at this point incapable of reciprocal relationship. The human spirit waits on human development to unfold its manifold operations.

Energy

Rooted in the organism, psychic energy, as I am presenting it here, is the dynamism of the human spirit *not yet aware of itself*. Grounded in the physicality of the human being, the energy is not even fully itself *psychically* at this point. This created life force drives the impetus in cell division from the very moment of conception. I believe also that human psychic energy is programmed to unfold in emotion, thinking, and choice from the start. In contrast to the life force in plants or even in animals, human psychic energy will not rest until consciousness emerges in its distinctive *self-reflexive* human form. From the beginning it presses forward until a heartbeat emerges, accompanying the impetus that orchestrates cell division, the unfolding of the design for each organ, and commits to psychic memory the feel of the interaction of these various systems even in utero. This energy, in its most physical form, is the instrumental cause of the start of fetal breathing, records the sounds and feeling tone of the mother, and imprints early sensations in the feeling memory. The role of this life force, this energy field, active in its psychic form in the development of the human organism, is only beginning to be explored in prenatal science.[1]

The dimension of the human that identifies this psychic energy and its orchestration of the shaping of the physical organs, physical functions, and synchronized physical systems I am calling the "body." The role of psychic energy in physicality is important. To ignore it is to dismiss the psychosomatic interconnections becoming more evident in medicine and mental health with each passing day.

But psychic energy is not confined to organic functions. Psychic energy in itself is the object of study and research. In its functions of imaging and emoting, fantasizing and dreaming, psychic energy is manifested in animals and humans both. The type of consciousness

---

[1] One source of this information is a set of nine tapes available from the Pre- and Perinatal Psychology Association of North America, recording presentations made at its Fifth International Congress July 18–21, 1991, in Atlanta, Georgia (Boulder, CO: Sounds True Recordings, 1992).

it presses for in humans, however, is distinctive. The degree of self-reflexivity evident in humans is different from types of consciousness present in animals. How do we know? The empirical evidence rests upon observation and analysis of *functioning*. Consciousness in humans operates with different and more complex functions than those observed in animals. Humans not only form images; they decide which images they will entertain and which they will suppress.

In the human, psychic energy blossoms into the experience of self-awareness accompanied by wonder. Wonder leads to curiosity and questioning. Questioning results in reflecting on data, and finally, the reflecting on facts turns to a reflecting on the worth of something, its value. This psychic energy, rooted in the physical and pressing forward toward the human capacity to think and choose, fuses the entire range of human operations into a unified whole. The psychic energy itself and the highly developed human functions of thinking and choosing I am calling the "soul."

In what we have identified as the *body*, the psychic energy is limited to physical and psychological functions. In what we have identified as the *soul*, psychological and cognitive functions distinguish the human from functions shared with the animal. Said another way, I am suggesting the *human* soul is a life principle (energy) capable of the functions that lead to the operations of self-reflective thought and choice. The human is a triple composite. As organism, psyche, and spirit, this three-twoness is a composite of matter and spirit permeated and fused by psychic energy.

If this is what humanness is, it is precisely what was joined to the divine Word in what we call the "hypostatic union." What is human in this union is human, not divine, and what is divine in this union is divine, not human. As Athanasius reminds us, they are not "mixed." They are two distinct realities fused, never to be separated. The human functions humanly. The Divine functions divinely. In ourselves it is this humanness, in its human functioning, that will interact with the Divine in the divine self-giving we call "grace." The question remains: *How* will the Divine interact with the human while allowing, and even prompting, the human to fully function, indeed to flourish in its own created reality?

Tension

There is normal *tension* involved in this embodied spirit or spiritual embodiment. Psychic energy as it interacts with physicality is met with constant limitation (see diagram 1, page 113). The energy as it sublates[2] and begins to function cognitively and rationally moves as though guided by some unseen hand toward the unending possibility of further transcendence. As the eye begins at the left of diagram 1 and moves to the right, the dynamism of the energy as sublating can be sensed in a limited way. The dynamic energy itself as sublating can only be conceptualized in active functioning. It is not a static reality as depicted.

As with the human sperm, driven on to seek its goal with unremitting urgency, the human psychic energy presses onward to more complex functions. Linking our two hands in a hand lock is a good physical example of the balance needed between human limitation and transcendence. The tension of the hand lock is maintained only if each arm pulls in its own direction. If the tension is broken, the balance is lost. Breaking the tension in the direction of embodiment can result in addiction, the bondage to food, drink, chemicals, or sex that makes physical dependence a prison of limits. Breaking the tension in the direction of transcendence, with little or no thought of human limitation, results not in holiness but in psychosis: the loss of a sense of boundary.

Evidence of the psychotic is often found in the painful loss of a sense of limits. The remedy for the imbalance stuck in compulsive addiction is *new possibility*. For the person lost in possibility and planning, the remedy is a *concrete grounding* in reality. Either dysfunctional condition is detrimental to a sound spirituality. To be truly human is to be in a balanced tension of limitation and transcendence, a balance negotiated by a psychic energy that drives onward toward constant negotiations between a plethora of functions: physical, psychic, and spiritual. The orchestration of these functions gradually reveals more heightened human operations.

This is no dualism, but it is a clear duality and distinction of human function. The energy drives of the physical organism have in the past been pitted *against* the human drive toward transcendence. There have been times when a frenzied fervor for mortification of the body assumed that our physicality had a mind of its own and was out to get us. Bent on our spiritual ruin, human physicality was subjected to untold abuse in the name of God. A mistaken reading of Paul's use of

---

[2] This term, used by Karl Rahner and Bernard Lonergan, refers to the ever-transcending capacity of the human spirit. A higher level of operation *sublates* a lower; that is, retaining what was possible at the former level, the higher level shows a heightened functional capacity. Nothing is lost. What was possible is enhanced with more possibility.

the term *sarx* (flesh) equated *sarx* with *soma* (body). The body was brutalized to subdue the heart of flesh and its sinful impulses. It is a surprise to some to learn that the seat of sin is in the *choices* one makes, and choice is a function of the human *spirit*, not of the organism. The body in reality often becomes a mere accomplice to a crime already committed in the decision one has made. This is not to say the organism doesn't have its own needs and make them known in no uncertain terms, but decisions lie elsewhere. It is the human spirit that decides whether the organism gets what it wants or is to be deferred in pursuit of a greater good.

The physical dimension of the human being in all its wondrous complexity is known best by those who know its intricacies: the surgeons, the lab technicians, and the anatomy specialists. In spirituality these sciences and the knowledge they reveal become a source of wonder. Energy in its physical form is humble and limited even as it is wondrous. The mysteries of the double helix, of DNA, of chromosomal and genetic structures, and of enzymes and proteins hold fragile secrets begging to be told. The body grows tired. It hungers and thirsts. It knows illness, malfunction, and decay. It is no wonder that in some religious traditions the goal is to rid oneself of its demands, deprive it of its needs, and beat it into numbness.

Sexuality

The incarnation as the central pattern of this study points in another direction. Physicality is a necessary and vital means of communication for the human spirit. The body, in its physicality, is sacramental. It mediates the soul's longings, dreams, hopes, ideas, conclusions, and decisions to the surrounding world. We are called to steward the physical, to shepherd it, direct it, curb it, and comfort it. The energy most obvious and often most feared in the body is sexual energy. Experienced physically as a deeply rooted "skin hunger," this longing for intimacy with the human is so basic to survival that it has been identified by Freudians as the most primitive of human drives. But we should be suspicious. While sexual energy is manifesting itself so clearly as a drive toward physical intimacy, is the physical its real source? What if the real seat of sexual energy is the human spirit, and physical erotic desire is the instrument by which its song is sung?

We have already proposed that psychic energy itself is the ground of the human soul, rooted in the Divine. It is the first manifestation of the presence of human life. What may be novel is the possibility that sexuality's drive toward intimacy is the primary powerful form this energy takes. If this is so, then sexual energy is part of, and one with, the drive toward transcendence. It carries the human person beyond the protection of an isolated, self-enclosed security. Restoring sexual longing to its rightful place in the midst of the human thrust toward self-transcendence heals a painful dislocation. Alignment with the longing for transcendence gives sexual energy the respect due to it and at the same time honestly points out the limits of its physical expression. Sexual energy always points to something more. Intimacy with the human is the precursor to intimacy with the Divine. It is meant to be a preview of coming attractions.

No one would deny that the human is a creature of desire, of longing. The most basic human longing is not for sex but for *intimacy*. That genital sex is a psychosomatic means to realize this longed-for intimacy raises eyebrows. The desire to be recognized, to be known, to be with, to be accepted, to belong, to be touched, to be held, to be united with—all this urging is toward some form of intimacy. If genital sexual activity is one way to attain such intimacy, are there other ways? Why do the mystics describe intimacy with the Holy in terms of sexual imagery? Sexual longing draws us out of ourselves. When the goal of the longing for intimacy is expressed in genital sexual intimacy with another human being, the activity is no less self-transcending. With those who choose a celibate expression, that same energy presses on to another goal. It may be creative expression in service of others or in an art form such as painting or dance, or perhaps the passion begs expression in writing. When sexual energy settles for no less than intimacy with the Holy, its expression often takes the form of profound compassion. Whatever form it takes, the urgency of sexual energy propels the human beyond herself or himself. The energy manifests itself in varied ways, but there will be a central focus. For some it is an absorption in the pursuit of the Holy so profound that the need for human intimacy moves to the background. Celibate contemplatives will avow that genital sexual intimacy would distract them from the Mystery that captivates their attention. When the thrust to human intimacy is the focus, couples will avow that their genital sexual intimacy is a threshold to an experience of the Divine. Intimacy with the Holy and the human—fired by one and the same energy—rests only when that intimacy in some way is realized.

It is sad to note in our time that desecrating the need for intimacy with the Holy or with the human can bring the human being to its knees. The manipulation of religion and sexuality accounts for much of the violence that plagues our personal relationships, our cities, our nation, and our world. Pedophilia, the pornography market, prostitution, marital infidelity, fundamentalism, holy war, inquisition, silencing, excommunication, Jonestown, Waco, Heaven's Gate—all bear testimony to the abuse of this longing for intimacy with the human and the Holy. What is not understood is that the human body becomes accomplice and victim in these activities and that the crime originates elsewhere. The crime is birthed in the human spirit, in its capacity to make poor choices in its quest for true intimacy.

The role of genital sexuality in spirituality needs open and honest discussion, not the silence that has surrounded it in the past. The body in its genital sexual expression is one piece with the sacramental sense of the physical as mediating the total self of the person to the world. When understood in its richness, sexuality is a distinct language of the soul, not merely a physical/emotional need. Rather than merely psychosomatic, sexuality needs to be treated also as psychospiritual, an expression of the total human being. Sexual energy seeks expression. Genital expression is but one means of communication.

Genital sexual expression comes into its own only when it says what it means and means what it says. As with other forms of communication, it can lie. It is true when it speaks an intimacy both sought and realized. As sought and realized, it is a language meant to communicate the whole self, not a self reduced merely to bodily function. A minimalist perspective on human sexuality narrows it to bodily activity or refraining from such activity. A sacramental sense of the body prompts us to understand genital sexual expression as the gift of a total person to another person. A more adequate understanding will locate sexual activity where it really originates: in the deepest longings of the human soul seeking communion. The human hunger for intimacy will be satisfied only with personal relationship with the human and with the Holy. The mere consideration of these two longings as one *within* the other goes a long way to heal the guilt-laden fear that has surrounded sexual longing. Such consideration opens the way for authentic sexual delight and celebration.

When human sexual longing is divorced from its deeper thirst for the Holy, dislocation sets in. Human skin hunger tends to go off whoring. It has become an end in itself. Prostituted sexual energy must survive on the scraps of passing pleasure. But the real feast, the heady wine of sexual wholeness, is found in the relational communion of two people. The intimacy is fed from their relationship, and the body plays host and acts as sanctuary. Sexual activity in the context of the thirst for the Holy is indeed a form of worship. The Holy is met and honored in the beloved. As a result, its pleasure blossoms into true joy.

We have been considering psychic energy as it functions *psychosomatically*. It is this same energy functioning *psychospiritually* that we now need to explore. This will mean a further clarification of what we mean by the human psyche and its functions. What are the functions of psychic energy when it is not yet conscious? What empirically changes when it becomes conscious? How does it manifest itself at the threshold of consciousness, when it functions in its own realm—when it functions simply *psychically*?

The Human Psyche

Psychic Functions

The approach taken here is limited. It is not the approach of the psychoanalyst. It will remain for psychologists and clinicians to comment on and critique what is proposed here. The approach taken here is drawn from the insights of several scholars whose works will appear in the bibliography: Thomas Aquinas, Bernard Lonergan, Robert M. Doran, Tad Dunne, Daniel A. Helminiak, and Sebastian Moore, among others less well known.

Again we need to clarify that we are not discussing *parts* of the human being. The human psyche is not a *part* of the human being. The human being is a unified whole. This whole has dimensions and distinctive *functions* that identify which dimension of the human is being considered. But it is a disservice to reduce the human to material parts, likening persons to machines. The human psyche is an energy field. The energy manifesting itself psychically differs from that same energy driving cellular division or prompting a bodily infection to heal, and it differs from the functions that will identify the cognitive and volitional operations of the human spirit.

Psychic energy as psychic is identified as feeling, as emoting, as dream symbolizing, as imaging, as imagining or linking images, as fantasizing. Alongside these explicit psychic manifestations, the energy effects, absorbs, and records bodily functioning in psychic memory. The psyche holds memories the mind knows not. In this feeling memory, the psyche as well as the human organism shares similarities with animals. Animals feel, they dream and imagine, and they remember psychically through an emotional or feeling memory. We all can recall animals cowering because of past abuse.

Emotions are powerful energy motors. What this means and how emotions work are of great interest today. Emotional intelligence is being discussed openly, and studies in the emotional similarity between humans and animals can be viewed on an ordinary evening on PBS. Of special interest in a study of spirituality is how psychic energy functions when it reaches the point of manifesting itself as an actual emotion.

Emotion

Although distant historically from our own time when psychology has become a discipline, Aquinas drew from the insights of Aristotle regarding human emotion.[3] The majority of writers dealing with emotion today take a more fragmented approach with no seeming knowledge of the careful observation of human functioning found in these early masters. I will incorporate insights from the Aristotelian/ Thomistic classification because it not only resonates with current work on human emotion but also provides a coherent system for the ongoing study of emotion, in contrast to the more eclectic treatment of some modern authors.

The distinction between *feeling* and what I will refer to as *emotion* is made clear by Lonergan.[4] He uses the word "feeling" to refer to *nonintentional states* such as hunger and tiredness arising from bodily conditions. Lonergan then discusses the role of feeling in *intentional response* and proceeds to unfold a nuanced explanation of human emotion as it "gives intentional consciousness its mass, momentum, drive, power."[5] My intent here is even more basic. It is to present the classical categories of human emotion as a starting point, fully aware that those more knowledgeable in the psychological field will be able to amplify these considerations in a more comprehensive and nuanced way. What is more important, we need to be sure the emotions are never again

---

[3] In qq. 22–48 of I-II of the *Summa Theologiae*, it is clear that Thomas is following Aristotle's classification of human passion or emotion. Clinical psychiatrist Conrad Baars, MD, and others explicitly refer to this classification in their practice, while others approach emotion without reference to this early classification.

[4] See *Method in Theology* (London: Darton, Longman and Todd, 1972), 30–34.

[5] Ibid., 30.

neglected in our efforts to shape an anthropology that is adequate for a consideration of spirituality that is both holistic and holy.

The classical approach identifies eleven basic human emotions in two main groups: *spontaneous* emotions and those more *considered*. (Thomas will use the terms "concupiscible" and "irascible.") The spontaneous emotions are identified in three pairs, each pair influencing the pair to follow. Thus *love* and *hate* lead to *desire* and *aversion* and culminate in either *joy* or *sadness*. In the sequence, love leads to desire, and if the object of the love is obtained, there is joy. In the other sequence, hate leads to aversion, and if what is despised must be endured, there is sadness or sorrow. These emotions, so named because they refer more to the "sensual appetite," arise spontaneously from information drawn from what is sensed bodily (see diagram 1).

The five considered emotions, *courage, fear, hope, despair*, and *anger*, are so named because there is more cognitional activity involved in them. *Courage* and *fear* appear in the face of challenge; *hope* and *despair* (powerlessness or impotency, not the vice) are experienced as possibility is assessed; *anger*, which has no opposite, flows from threat and prompts either fight or flight, depending on the situation.

What is interesting in the face of more modern classification is the fact that therapists working in mental health today will use the key words "glad," "sad," "mad," or "scared" to help their clients identify their basic emotional states. Two of these terms refer to spontaneous emotions, and two to considered emotions in the above classification. It is my conviction that this early classification still holds a valid starting place for acquiring self-knowledge and should not be easily dismissed as more recent emotional work is explored.

To neglect emotion in spiritual development is to court trouble. Psychic energy as it manifests itself in this powerful way is not to be ignored or repressed. Not dealt with, it is the hidden enslavement that can cripple intelligence and paralyze choice. What we call "memory" is often more emotional than cognitive. We remember how things *felt* more keenly than we remember facts about them, and that memory can abort images that might foster creative thought.

Psychic Scarring

From the work of Robert M. Doran, who wrote on the psyche, its blockage, and its healing, we learn that this sensitive energy field can become scarred. We need to keep in mind that in the human this energy becomes self-reflexively *conscious* of its own functioning when it comes into awareness. It is *aware*, but more importantly for humans, *it is aware that it is aware*. Because human consciousness is self-reflexive, two-way, not only one-way as it may be in animals, we can attend to what we are experiencing. In fact, when we are really attentive, we are addressing, not repressing, what we feel.

In addition to the psychic energy manifested in powerful emotions, the psyche stores images. What is seen, heard, felt, smelled, and touched is stored in the feeling memory, accompanied often by images that trigger emotion, whether they arise in dreams or by deliberate recall in therapy or in prayer. In fact, this is exactly what therapy does. It brings what has been repressed back into consciousness to be dealt with so that its power to keep us emotionally sick is defused.

Lonergan calls affect-laden images "symbols."[6] Whether the psyche is dealing with simple images brought in through the senses or with powerfully emotive symbols, this energy in a human being becomes conscious when we have bridged from the psychic field as such to the first level of the human *spirit*, conscious experience. As explained here, the psychic field is the joiner of the operations of body function with the operations of the human spirit. Grounded in the organism, psychic energy draws all the data picked up there into conscious inquiry and reflection. It grounds the soul (the operations of the spirit plus this energy field) in the body yet provides a way for us to distinguish psychic operation from the cognitive and evaluative operations of the full human spirit. The distinction of psyche and spirit is important for a thematic and systematic approach to the study of spirituality.

The Human Spirit

We have addressed the reality of the human organism with its complex systems, as well as the phenomenon of the human psyche with its capacity for storing feeling and emotion and with its ability to image. We have proposed that psychic energy orchestrates the functions of the human organism and prompts the unfolding of the operations of the human spirit. In identifying the functions distinct to the organism and those particular to the psyche, and contrasting these to the operations we will name "spiritual" in the human, we remove some of the ambiguity

---

[6] Ibid., 64.

in the language we need to use. It remains now for us to clarify what we mean by the human spirit. What is it? What are the operations of the human spirit? Are they truly human, or are they divine—something godly in us? Is the human spirit the proverbial "ghost in the machine"? Or is our human spirit as natural to us as our hair and eyelashes? I would offer here that we can indeed identify operations that pertain to the human spirit and that we can distinguish these operations from those we have already identified as physical or psychic. I propose also that the operations that identify the human spirit functioning in us are as natural as the smile on a child's face.

By "human" I am referring to what we ordinarily experience, understand, and know about ourselves. We experience ourselves as physical and emotional beings that think and choose. Not all of us identify the thinking and choosing as distinctly *spiritual* functions, and many of us would not identify what we name as "spiritual" as constitutive to being human. "Spiritual" is often thought of immediately as related to religion or to the Divine. The Divine, as we are using it here, pertains to God. It pertains to what originates in God, what God does, and how God acts upon the human being. The Divine is distinct from the human, just as the human is distinct from the Divine. But the human will settle for nothing less than intimacy with this Divine, and, remarkably, the Divine is more intent on this union than we are.

The methodological study of spirituality needs to attend to this commingling. A methodological approach needs to clarify, distinguish, and then attempt to relate and synthesize. Up to this point we have been clarifying what we mean by the human as an organism and by the human in its dynamic psychic energy field. How then shall we clarify what we mean by the human spirit, distinguishing it from both organism and psychic energy yet relating it to both?

Diagram 2, page 114, is a sketch of the human spirit as a whole. While grounded in the functions of the organism, the sensitive psyche is pictured by the words "sensitive" and "intelligent" because the psychic energy takes manifold forms in those operations we name as humanly and naturally spiritual. The elements of diagram 2 will be discussed in what follows in this study. The arrows superimposed on the four levels (circles) depict the psychic energy field in its own right, without reference to the organism or the spirit. The outermost circle (level 1) pictures the psychic energy transposing from data of physical functioning in the human to the most basic level of the human spirit, the level of conscious experience. The senses are indicated, and the level is identified as level 1 of the human spirit. But underpinning all, and foundational to what it means to be human, is the peak or depth of the soul called the "apex."

The Apex

Before the other levels of human operation are discussed, it will be important for us to address the very center of diagram 2. Identified as the "apex," the term begs explanation. Lonergan uses the term *apex animae* and describes it as the peak of the soul, "the ground and root of the fourth and highest level of man's intentional consciousness." This depth or height is the point of entry and indwelling of God's self-gift in love.[7] Although Lonergan has used the term in reference to intentionality analysis, the idea is not new. It appears in the writings of the early mystics and often takes on the rich imagery of the history of the time of its use. Catherine of Siena refers to the "cell" of the heart.[8] Teresa of Avila speaks of the "innermost room of the castle" to refer to this inner point of divine encounter.[9] From their own religious experience the mystics speak of a deep center indwelt by God (see diagram 3, page 115). They describe a hidden depth where the Divine is found shrouded in the darkness or opaqueness of faith in the midst of mundane activities. We will refer to this point of union with the Creator as the "apex" and propose that what flows from it is the human creature's very existence or being. This means that our being as human is grounded in and takes its origin from this Mystery.

What we are referring to here is a divine contact or permeation point in the human. In such a reference we need to be careful lest we think of this point of entry as a place located somewhere in our head, heart, forehead, or any bodily location. Can we really confine the Divine to a place where that presence influences our power to think and choose? Is the Holy to be located in the head because we experience ourselves thinking through the brain? Or is the Mystery present in what we call our "heart," because we consider the heart the center of loving? This attempt may be as futile as visualizing where our human spirit is located.

---

[7] Ibid., 107.

[8] See Mary Ann Fatula, OP, *Catherine of Siena's Way*, The Way of the Christian Mystics series, vol. 4 (Collegeville, MN: Liturgical Press, 1990 [1987]), 76–91.

[9] See Teresa of Avila, *The Interior Castle* (New York: Paulist, 1979), 172–82.

We find ourselves dangerously close to being back to the unhelpful notion of our soul as the ghost in the machine. What we propose is that the mystery of the human's own being wells up from the Divine, that without the Divine we are *not*. Further, we are coming to understand that this flow is manifested in an energy that takes various forms. Life energy as it mutates has the potential of stimulating physical genetic unfolding, psychic sensitivity, and those spiritual operations that identify the creature as distinctly human. The source is divine. The functioning is human. The human is made from nothing but the Love that is this Mystery. It has no existence without relation to this Mystery. The human center or "ground" of entry and the operations that we identify as spiritual operations in the created human are precisely that—human and created. Thus, the human spirit is a *human* reality. The human spirit is constitutive to being human; it is not some divine addition. It is in this human spirit, in its manifold operations, that the encounter with the Holy is possible. *What is the action of the Divine* on this human creature?

Experiencing

First, we *experience* reality, whether that reality is the ocean, a rose, a cat, a baby, or the divine Mystery itself. A *religious* experience is experience of the Divine at this peak of the soul. When the Divine moves in the conscious awareness of the human, we *experience* something. We rarely *understand* what we are experiencing, and so we do not *know* what it is. The experience may not be named "religious," because the person having the experience may not be familiar with such language. The person senses something (Someone?) in its horizon of awareness that was not there before. The experience, needless to say, is going to make a difference. We will deal with this kind of experience more fully later when we discuss religious conversion, but we bring it up here because this experience can create a distinct *foundation*[10] or viewpoint within which all cognition and choice will go on. Religious faith is a knowing born from the movement of this divine Love grasping the soul. For the believer it is *faith* in the reality of the Mystery as *experienced* that distinguishes the believer's viewpoint from that of the unbeliever. Faith is not a knowing that comes from rational exercise. The *state* or *condition* of being that comes about as a result of this encounter is the state of *being in love*, understood far beyond its usual erotic meaning. The Mystery

---

[10] See "Foundations" in Lonergan, *Method in Theology*, 267–93.

as Love has presented itself, and as a result one finds oneself actually *in that Love*, when before the encounter one was not. We need only recall the fact of the difference in me when I am romantically in love and when I am not. Tommy, quarterback on the high school football team, comes home from practice, comes into the kitchen, and gives his mom a peck on the cheek as she works at the stove. Smelling him before she sees him, she shoos him away with "To the shower with you!" But one afternoon Tommy comes in all shiny and showered and with his hair combed. Mom's comment to the peck on the cheek today is "What's her name?" Today Tommy is in love. He wasn't yesterday. This new state of being for Tommy captures what we are referring to, and just as Tommy responds to it with a change in behavior, so does the human now respond in love to God. We experience ourselves as different when we are in love. We experience ourselves at the center, and the Mystery of the Holy is now very much in our awareness. It wasn't before.

We can experience ourselves simply *experiencing*. So subtle is this first level of consciousness that we need to call attention to it so that we can become aware of it. To *notice* it is to *attend* to it. To do so is to *intend* to pay attention to our first level of conscious operation. It is simply to be *aware*. The imperative of the self-transcending energy at this first level of the human consciousness is "Attend! Notice! Be Aware! Be attentive!" The consciousness gapes in wonder at a sunset, at a baby's sleeping face, at a sense of presence in the center of the soul. At this basic preconceptual level it is important to note that we are not yet wondering about our wonder. We are simply *experiencing* it.

The Mystery of the Holy, experienced at the apex of the soul, is the experience of a contemplative consciousness. In Lonergan's terms it is a mystical *differentiation* of consciousness. It is the human consciousness highly differentiated to be in a state of awareness of the Divine, and the differentiation is becoming steadily more permanent. In relation to artistic form, movement, color, or texture, we might speak of an *aesthetic* or artistic differentiation of consciousness. In relation to careful, detailed scholarly work, we would speak of a *scholarly* differentiation of consciousness.

Understanding

When we wonder about our wondering, or begin to *question* what we wonder about, consciousness has shifted. What identifies the second level of consciousness is questioning for an understanding of our experience. We ask, "What is this?" or "Why did this happen?" or "Who can this be?" The energy prompts the imperative "Ask! Find out! Inquire! Be intelligent!" The consciousness feels different because it *is* different. It is busy examining the data we have experienced at level 1 and inquiring into it in order to identify what has been presented. It begins the process we identify as trying to reach *understanding*. As the data is questioned, notions are formed by pulling in former images and bits of images. Pieces are connected by the consciousness as they seem to fit. Pieces that make sense together suddenly "click," and the "Aha!" of insight erupts in consciousness. Insights coalesce and become concepts, and concepts gather to form ideas. This is the second level of conscious operation in diagram 2, the level of intelligent understanding.

Judging

The second level leaves us with scattered insights. We have our collection of bright ideas. But the consciousness is not satisfied. Haunting questions occur: "Is this bright idea a *right* idea? Are my insights correct? Are they true? Are some *more true* than others?" The energy once again prods, "Check them! Compare them! Question them further! Don't conclude too easily! Be reasonable!" The consciousness begins another set of operations, identified this time by the push and pull of contrast and comparison as to *truth content*. The process is that of arriving at *judgment*, the "Yes!" that comes after reflection on a variety of insights: "Yes, these are the facts. This is where truth lies." Most important for our overall understanding of the operations of human consciousness is the realization that *knowing* is reached only at this point. Experiencing is not knowing; it is merely experiencing. It is the first level of knowing. Understanding is not knowing; it provides the insights necessary for knowing. It is merely the second level of knowing. Knowing is concluding that an insight is *correct*, that it is *true*. Then and only then do I fully know. Until this point I am growing in understanding but have not yet reached the judgment that my understanding is correct.[11]

Intentionality analysis reveals that the dynamism that keeps this movement going is cyclic and recurrent. If new data is experienced at level 1, the consciousness is drawn to include it and begin again.

---

[11] Bernard Lonergan, *Collected Works of Bernard Lonergan,* vol. 3: *Insight: A Study of Human Understanding* (Toronto: University of Toronto Press, 1992 [1957]), 381.

Hopefully, this brief sketch describes human intelligence in action, in the dynamism that it is. Human intelligence will not rest until it *knows*. This drivenness or orientation of the human spirit Lonergan calls the "pure desire to know."[12] It is cool, detached, disinterested, and unrestricted. This is the third level of conscious operation in diagram 2, the level of reasonable judgment. Anthropologically, the question of *why* the consciousness moves in this way is grounded in the very makeup of the human spirit. The human longs to know the truth and will not rest until it does. The human spirit in its inner dynamism is made for truth.

Deciding

Once we have arrived at knowing, the consciousness is now satisfied, right? Wrong. The consciousness again shifts and is prodded still further. Now no longer questioning for understanding or for truth, the questions become questions of *value*. "So what if this is true? What difference does it make? What's it worth to you? What do you intend to do about it?" The shift is from the *truth* of the matter to the *value* of what is at stake. The consciousness in its operations is moving from the intellectual levels to the level of choice and action, the level of *decision* (level 4 in diagram 2). The process here is one of evaluation, of questioning for the comparative worth and effect of a possible choice. Here what we identify as *conscience* emerges—formed, informed, or deformed, depending on how *attentive*, *intelligent*, and *reasonable* the person has been up to this point. The urging of the energy is "Check the results! Look for the impact! Be responsible!" A decision is pending, a choice is to be made, and action or refraining from action will follow. The person has hopefully been attentive, intelligent, reasonable and now will be *responsible*.

We have completed a sketch of the operations of human consciousness. In doing so, we have charted the operations of the distinctly human spirit. That human spirit, together with the psychic energy that prods it, we have named the distinctly human "soul." It now remains for us to ask the simple questions "Is this what I do? Is this how I come to know something? Is this what I do when I am moving toward a good decision?" In offering us this charting, Lonergan enables us to glimpse

---

[12] References to Lonergan's use of this expression abound in his writings. See *Insight*, 372–76, for one such discussion.

the operations of the human spirit. But in asking us whether this is what we do, he is inviting us to *self-appropriation*, the self-assessment that will put us in touch with our own conscious operations. Once we come to know ourselves in how our own consciousness functions, we become capable of *intentionality analysis*, the ability to experience, understand, and judge our own conscious operations with the hope of being able to direct them intentionally. Held in the creative love of God, this is entering into one's self; it is being in possession of one's soul. To our knowledge today, the capacity to intentionally direct these operations distinguishes the human from the animal. This capacity gives us an approach to intelligence and free choice that is functional and empirical, for we can begin to direct our own conscious operations. We can make the operations of our consciousness the object of our attention. By this Lonergan means we can *intentionally* experience, understand, judge, and evaluate our own human operations. By careful attentiveness we can come to know ourselves and can more intentionally direct those operations, notice when we omit them, and be on our guard against the biases that cripple them. If this is an accurate charting of the operations of the human spirit, then skill in intentionality analysis has everything to do with the development and growth of the human spirit and thus with spirituality, for it is in and through the human spirit that we have access and relationship with the Holy.

If we are honest, we often think we know, but in truth we know only partially. We think we have others sized up, but we are wrong. This human spirit we have charted doesn't always function attentively, intelligently, reasonably, and responsibly. Why not? What is it that cripples us, that prevents us from operating as the spiritual beings we are? It is to a consideration of what can *shut down* the human spirit in its authentic operation that we now turn.

Vectors, Biases, and Imperatives

The marvel of the human dynamic that we have described is sobered by the realization that it doesn't always work the way it's intended. Diagram 2 looks so static and cohesive with levels of conscious operation centered around the apex, the level of transcendence. But before we try to understand what blocks the operations, we need to clarify the drawing power or orientation of the energy itself. Psychic energy sublates from the lower levels to the higher levels as the operations heighten their activity, finally reflecting cognitional and volitional functioning. We also need to be clear that the pull can also be in the opposite direction, from value and choice to a deepened understanding and new experience.

Lonergan uses the term "vector" to describe this twofold pull. Diagram 2 introduces vectors into the imagery. The vector that draws the human consciousness to work for solutions from data to decision is called "creative." It works inward to the core, from experience through inquiry and from judgment to decision. The vector that works from the core outward and releases the consciousness from whatever cripples its operation is called "healing." The healing is for the creating; the activity of one in human consciousness affects the activity of the other.[13] What is healed allows for the creative flow from below. The creative flow can continue until it is further blocked or hindered. What blocks the operations of human consciousness?

The breakdown of the recurrent pattern of human consciousness is brought about by *bias*. Lonergan identifies four types of bias, or *scotosis*.[14] Likened to a painful callus in the physical realm, scotosis is a rigidity or "stuckness" in the forward dynamism of the psychic energy. *Dramatic bias* affects the first level of operation, the level of experience, by compromising the imperative to be attentive. Arising out of the drama of traumatic life experience, dramatic bias can effectively limit the emergence of *images arising in the psyche*. Acting like a psychic callus or scarring, dramatic bias restricts the free flow of images from the psychic memory. Images that recall a painful experience are censored by a type of psychic "policing." As a result of this censorship, the images needed for new insights are selectively withheld because they are fraught with pain or fear. The release comes with good therapy, or the dissolving of the resistance through intense human love, or the purifying love of God that is experienced in contemplative prayer often accompanied by tears.

Individual bias restricts honest questioning for new insight. Individual egoism refuses to admit there might be truth outside its own understanding of it. You have nothing to tell me. There is nothing I can learn from you. When this closed-mindedness becomes corporate,

---

[13] Again, these terms appear in several places in Lonergan's writings. A primary reference is "Healing and Creating in History," in *Third Collection*, ed. Frederick E. Crowe (New York: Paulist, 1985), 100–109.

[14] A discussion of bias appears briefly in the previous reference. A more developed treatment can be found in Lonergan's *Insight* as listed in the index.

we recognize *group bias* at work. We are familiar with this mind-set. Our race is the only race, our gender is the only gender, our nation is number one, our religion alone has the truth. From group egoism is spawned the *isms* that infect individual consciousness and company policy: the superiority complex of racism, the gender arrogance of sexism, the judgmental dismissal of religious fundamentalism. Finally, there is the pervasive pall of *general* or *theoretic bias*. This restriction deems intellectual endeavor with its long-term results impractical. After all, pragmatic results are needed—now. This anti-intellectualism has no patience with dreamers and visionaries, artists and poets, and those who imagine how things might be. It is concerned only with immediate, pragmatic results.

If these biases go unrecognized, they can permeate the consciousness. When infected with unchecked bias, those who have power to make decisions can cripple a culture, infecting its infrastructure, its social fabric, and its human relations on every level. The result can be total cultural decline. An example is Germany under the influence of Hitler's anti-Jewish bias. In contrast, it is the exposure and dissolving of bias that allows reconciliation of differences, respect of diversity, and the establishment of peace.

There are a variety of psychological typologies that attempt to explain the human being and its distortions. Each of them has valuable insights to offer. Each of them has limitations. The determinist types insist the human is really not free. That the human is determined interiorly (Freud) or externally (Skinner) prompts a variety of schools following the teachings of their respective founders. There are the humanists who hold for real freedom yet insist the human must be explained on its own terms. Those who push for that explanation with no direct reference to the Divine are the *secular humanists* (Ellis, Jung), and those who seek to give an account for divine influence we might call *integrative humanists* (Frankl, Otto). Those who seriously try to give an account of consciousness in an interdisciplinary way, incorporating insights from the East, are developing the *transpersonal psychology movement* (Wilber, Assagioli). The careful consideration of the positions of these thinkers will be a growing critical need.[15]

---

[15] Chapters 3 and 4 of Helminiak's *Religion and the Human Sciences: An Approach via Spirituality* (New York: SUNY, 1998) are just such an attempt. Helminiak carefully analyzes the thought of Don Browning and Ken Wilber in light of the intentionality analysis suggested by Bernard Lonergan, and he points out contrasts.

What we have offered here is a distinct analysis that can be of service in evaluating other approaches. This analysis must be ready to be evaluated by them in turn. This careful work will be vital to careful methodical work in spirituality.

The *breakdowns* have been pointed out in terms of the four biases. It is also important to recall the *breakthroughs* that prod the consciousness to function as it was intended. We identified the *imperatives* earlier as we explored the shifts from level to level in consciousness. It will do well to revisit them here in summary. The dynamic, created energy of the human spirit is designed to operate on all four levels without hindrance. Lonergan refers repeatedly in his writings to the imperatives as urgencies in the consciousness designed to fulfill its authentic operations.

"Be attentive" is the imperative that calls for the full functioning of awareness on level 1. To what is one to be attentive? To the data of sense flooding in through the senses of the organism and to the data of consciousness itself as it notices its own awareness.

On level 2 the imperative "Be intelligent" prompts the questioning that searches out the meaning needed for understanding. What does one need to understand? One's own body, the government, the society, God. The content to be understood may vary, but the process the consciousness goes through to reach meaning will be the same. It will entail careful questioning until sufficient understanding is reached.

"Be reasonable" is the third-level imperative that calls for careful reflection on the understanding one has reached in order to arrive at the judgment of whether the understanding is correct. Is the meaning I arrived at accurate? Is the understanding true? Yes or no? The alternative to a reasonable judgment of fact is a *rash* judgment, one reached too quickly before all the pertinent questions have been explored.

Fourth-level operation is prompted by the imperative "Be responsible." It urges taking responsibility for what one chooses to do, and it takes seriously the agony and ecstasy of being able to make a decision. True freedom will consist in the authentic response to these four imperatives in seeking the good, not in the mere exercise of making a choice. The implications of understanding the vectors, biases, and imperatives for conscience formation would provide a challenging discussion. They will be at work as we explore moral conversion later in this study.

Be attentive to your experience; *be intelligent* in your questioning for understanding; *be reasonable* in your conclusions (judgments); *be responsible* for your decisions. To these imperatives, demanding the best from the human, we add a final imperative that bridges us into the second half of this study: "Be in love." Be in love above all with that Mystery that we name as divine. Be in love with others, who are other marvels as you are yourself. Be in love with the earth and all it holds. Be in love with the wonder of yourself, attempting to respond to the divine Truth that is Love. Be in love.

It is this human, as we have described it, that is to be in relation to the Divine. How does the Divine act in relation to this human, who is designed to function authentically as a human being? Will the Divine dispose of the human, push it aside, or engage it? It is now time to begin to probe into possible tentative answers to these questions.

Summary

1. An adequate anthropology for spirituality will need to include all facets of the human being: physicality, emotion, intelligence, and choice. The ambiguity of the body-mind-spirit triad prompts us to seek a more adequate anthropology. The human understood as organism, psyche, and spirit offers a more inclusive framework. In this framework the organism accounts for the physical aspects of humanness; the psyche encompasses the emotions and dream/image aspects, and the human spirit refers to the cognitive and volitional aspects of the human.

2. At the source of the human spirit is the apex, the core, the center of the human grounded in the Divine. This groundedness draws its being from Mystery and has no existence without relation to it. This ontological relationship is one of simple creation. Yet its fact is the basis for a mutual exchange of friendship between the Divine and the human.

3. The operations of the human spirit consist of experience, understanding, judgment, and decision. By means of these operations the human can be in a state of being in love—or being in God, who is personified Love—in its relation to all of creation.

4. The vectors are dynamic energy thrusts in human consciousness. The healing vector operates from the core downward or outward, dissolving bias and freeing the operations to creatively function. The creative vector operates from experience upward or inward, demanding authentic and unrestricted functioning on the experience, understanding, judgment, and decision levels of operation. The impetus of these vectors can be a *functional* explanation for the dynamics of sanctifying (healing) and actual (creating) grace.

5. The biases are forms of scotosis, or blockage of human functioning. *Dramatic bias* is psychic scarring. It acts as a psychic censor, restricting the emergence of images that are needed for new insights. When we are unconscious of it, dramatic bias affects the psychic field, blocking its dynamic flow. When one becomes aware of it, its ability to cripple the first level of consciousness can be dealt with through courage to face what has caused intense pain. *Individual bias, group bias*, and *general* or *theoretical bias* primarily affect level 2 of consciousness. Individual egoism selectively excludes new information and restricts inquiry to data acceptable to myself personally. Group egoism is a rejection of facts contrary to group selectivity of pertinent data. It restricts new insights and accepts only data to suit the group's own purposes. General bias is an anti-intellectualism that has no patience with long-term results. It is fixated upon the common sense status quo and immediate results.

6. The imperatives are self-transcending dynamic energy thrusts that keep the consciousness moving to yet higher levels of operation. The first, "Be attentive," urges attentiveness to our experiences. The second, "Be intelligent," urges careful questioning of what we have experienced. The third, "Be reasonable," urges careful judgment following upon the cessation of all pertinent questions. The fourth, "Be responsible," urges decision based on careful evaluation of the worth of the matter to be decided. A final imperative, "Be in love," is an urging to ground oneself in Mystery as a state of being.

CHAPTER FIVE

The Divine Foundation

Total Reality

We began this study with our own experience in this time in history. It is a time marked by a hunger for spirituality and a simultaneous disdain for organized religion. We also sketched briefly how we got to where we are in terms of spirituality. Being people of these times, some would have us stay with our experience and do our reflection only within its horizon. But *our* experience is not all there is. There is *your* experience, as well as the experience of those who have gone before us. My perspective on the truth is not absolute, nullifying all others. Your perspective on the truth is no more absolute than mine, making all others moot. The postmodern worldview would have us settle for this as the best we can expect. But a theotic viewpoint, the viewpoint that includes the presence of ultimate Mystery as personal, suggests there is more. There are the accumulated wisdom traditions of believers in every culture. These wisdom traditions point to a Mystery beyond our beck and call. They prick the balloon of an inflated anthropological arrogance. They summon us as a human family to begin with our humanness, yes, but to admit there is something more than ourselves. The theotic viewpoint posits that "something" as the context for full human flourishing.

Science itself has pointed out the limits of our empirical knowledge and experience.[1] What is visible to the eye is not all that is there. To

---

[1] On p. 10 of the Health and Science section of the *St. Louis Post-Dispatch* for Friday, June 20, 2003, the Associated Press offered some startling scientific information. Astronomers have concluded, the article announced, that all that is visible to us is less than 1 percent of the entire universe. To explain, the article went on to say that luminous matter—stars, planets, and hot gas—account for only about 0.4 percent of the universe; nonluminous components, such as black holes and intergalactic gas, make

pose that what is beyond the telescope or hidden from the microscope is real is to ask natural faith of the human being. This request for human faith is indeed natural; its object is human assent to what is credible. If we are honest, the majority of our life is lived on faith, not knowledge. We believe what Peter Jennings tells us on the evening news. We believe there is only 10 percent ethanol in the gas we pump into our cars. We believe the level of sodium indicated on the VanCamps pork and beans can at the store. We believe our doctor and our government officials—sometimes. We believe our bishop or our pastor—most of the time. I even believe the cars will stop as I step off the curb when the lights are in my favor. We don't *know* any of these things. We don't even have the time or ability to check them out. Without basic trust in the credibility of others, we would soon be on the brink of madness. And so we gamble. We gamble that others are telling us the truth. If they deceive us—rob us of our savings or con us into buying something falsely advertised—we become furious. They have betrayed our trust, and we become wary of taking someone's word the next time.

When we believe in Ultimate Reality, the object of our faith is now the divine Mystery. Our faith is now religious. *That we believe* is a decision of faith. *How we explain* that faith is *belief*, and religious faith and belief too are a gamble. The "real" now includes Something or Someone ultimate, beyond my human limits to understand or even experience in full. I *choose* to believe. My mind with its understanding is forever running—huffing and puffing—to keep up.

The wisdom traditions of the earth propose that there is a Reality beyond us, beyond what we see, touch, taste, hear, and smell. This Reality is not me. It is not like me. It is Something or Someone I will need to decide whether to relate to. If I choose to gamble and do so, I bind myself to the seeking of this Mystery. The intentional seeking sets me in the direction of using all my humanness in this pursuit, and now what was the simple spiritual development of my humanness becomes *religious*. But make no mistake: there is spiritual activity that is *not religious*. Wondering, questioning, reflecting, and evaluating—these are spiritual functions, and as far as we can determine right now, they are uniquely human *whether or not* they are religious.

---

up 3.6 percent. The rest is either dark matter, about 23 percent, or dark energy, about 73 percent. We owe our very existence to this dark matter, for without it there would be virtually no structures in the universe.

If I am a religious seeker with others and we agree on what we believe, how we will live, and how we will worship, a religion is born. I have decided to gamble on the existence of this Mystery and join with others who do likewise. But others may call me foolish—a dependent pietist. So they too gamble, but they throw their dice in another direction. It is the direction of nonbelief in such a Reality. God is nothing but a need-projection. The goal of human life is possession, success, or pleasure—nothing more. I need to believe only in myself and in my own clever ingenuity. Ethical behavior is helpful for people to get along, and if you cheat, just take care not to get caught at it. Beauty surrounds us—a happenstance of nature. Enjoy it while you can. Life is all too short. Death is final. There is nothing else.

Each of us must decide how we are going to gamble. Persons who dismiss religious faith must live with the gamble that they may come to the end of life and find they were utterly wrong. Believers must face the same possibility. The existence or nonexistence of this Mystery cannot be proven empirically either way, and no amount of need-projection will create it or uncreate it. And so we choose, each of us often trying to convince the other that we have made the better choice and pointing to the effects of our decisions. Those who believe and identify with a religion point out the heroes and heroines among them and are embarrassed at the brutality visited on others in the name of that same religion. Those who choose not to believe point out their independence from religious authority and publicize the evidence of their philanthropy—and so it goes. We watch, and what really impresses us is the *human beauty* we see unfolding. Nature's beauty holds us spellbound, but human beauty of body form and character charms us as nothing else can. It can move us to tears—believers and nonbelievers alike. Perhaps Dostoyevsky was right. The world will, in the end, be saved by beauty.

The reality of this "belief situation" in our time is stark. It is real. In our time religious faith is a choice more than it has been in the past, and it is quite *intentional* on the part of those who identify themselves as believers. We will gamble in the direction the wisdom traditions point to and hopefully give reasons for the faith that is in us as we proceed.

We begin by drawing from the wisdom tradition that is distinctly Judeo-Christian, and we identify ourselves honestly as Christian. Specifically, we will be drawing from the wisdom figures of this tradition, women and men known for their relationship with the Mystery—the holy ones. We will be drawing from the Scriptures and from writings of the mystics, people who have been religiously in love.

Energy and Grace-Life

Our probing of the human began with a brief consideration of energy. It is time again to return to that consideration. We need to ground that energy and identify its source from within the theotic viewpoint in which we stand. Both testaments offer us a clear identification. In the account of Moses before the burning bush the words "I AM" stand out (Exod 3:14). In the Gospel of John these same words are heard repeatedly on the lips of Jesus.[2] What the Christian wisdom tradition has long understood by these words is the identification of the Mystery with the One who is, the One who is transcendent being. This is no mere escape into metaphysics. It is the identification of the One from whom *all beings receive their existence.* This is the Real from whom all realities receive any realness they have. Knowing this Real brings us to the Truth, for *the true is the real as known by the mind.* We have our own perspectives on the truth of things. But this is *the* Truth from which comes any truth you or I happen to have. It is from this dynamic life source that any energy we have as human emerges. The energy that directs the development of the embryo, that orchestrates hormonal interaction, that sculpts cellular development, and that differentiates itself in the sensitive psyche flows from Ultimate Reality as water does from a spring.

It is not our purpose here to examine into the philosophical and theological positions drawn from these convictions. For now it is enough for us to know that the Christian tradition identifies the Divine with Ultimate Reality and understands that reality as the fullness of being and truth. But there is more. The Christian Scriptures identify God as Love (see 1 John 4:8).[3] The Love referred to here is the self-giving Love that offers itself without concern about a return—unconditional, agapic Love. So the Christian tradition presents to the world an Ultimate Reality/Truth that loves. Further, this Truth that loves comes seeking a relationship with the human creature, and we have described the anthropology of that creature in the last chapter.[4]

---

[2] E.g., John 6:35, 48; 8:12, 58; 9:5; 10:7; 11:25; 14:6; 15:1.

[3] In what follows, capitalized "Love" will refer to this identification with God.

[4] The Song of Songs in the First Testament is a passionate depiction of this search and has been interpreted as such in both the Jewish and Christian traditions. In the Gospel of John of the Second Testament, the public life of Jesus begins at a wedding in which the newly created wine is taken to the lesser bridegroom. The real bridegroom is Jesus, who in his person as divine Word has married humanness. It should not escape

So the Truth that loves comes courting. But that courtship will need to be the seduction of the human in the totality of its humanness. The Christian tradition that is ours needs to be held in tension with the three-dimensional human anthropology of the last chapter so that none of the richness escapes.

We can then posit a basic assumption about the Divine that we glean from the accumulated wisdom of the Scriptures and our community of faith: this Mystery is *Being itself, the Ultimate Reality, the Truth that loves.* If we are honest, we don't know this Mystery really. We do not possess it. Instead, it possesses us. My little beingness is held by it as the fish is held by the sea. I live and move in it as in an ocean of air.[5] The *fact* of this is one thing, and *my awareness* of it is another. I may be totally oblivious of the fact. It may be so, but I may neither know it nor relate to it. If I should experience this Mystery in myself, it might change everything.

We have located the creative presence of this "fact" at the core of our being in our discussion of the apex. When this Mystery moves in the human heart, however, the Mystery comes into the person's horizon of awareness. *We become conscious of it.* It was missing from my conscious horizon, and now it is there. I drive and come up over a hill. Suddenly, a mountain enters into my horizon of vision; it was there all the while—*but not in my horizon of awareness.* So it is with initial religious experience. This Mystery may make its presence known in a myriad of ways. A presence felt as I walk in the woods—I pause, and it is gone. I shake my head and muse, "What was that?" I may not even have any religious language to name it. The presence may make itself known as I stand gazing down at my son's body in the casket at the funeral parlor. The Other has intruded into my awareness, and I am strangely comforted. I may not have any religion. I may not even be a "believer" in the usual religious sense.

Religious experience may not be *understood* or *known* as religious, but the experience will not be easily forgotten, and it is more common

---

notice that in the passion narrative of John's gospel we have a poignant declaration of Jesus: "I am thirsty" (19:28). This is the cry of God made flesh. For what could that God possibly thirst, if not for the saving relationship so sought?

[5] See Catherine of Siena, *The Dialogue*, trans. Suzanne Noffke, OP (New York: Paulist, 1980), 112: "Just as the fish is in the sea and the sea in the fish, so am I in the soul and the soul in me, the sea of peace."

than we want to admit in a secular society.[6] The person is capable of the experience because the person is *spiritual*. The spiritual constitution of the human being is made for this interaction. Some have said we are "wired" for communication with this Mystery. Religions attempt to give voice to this experience in the persons of their holy ones and mystics.

The language used by Christians to name the personal relationship of this Mystery with the human is "grace." It comes gently, unnoticed by the child sleeping through its own baptism. It can overpower, bringing a convert to tears. The language used to name the entrance of this Mystery into the human awareness is "religious experience." It is experience, the first level of consciousness, but experience of the very ground that underpins all human functioning. It is experience *at the apex*. The human consciousness wakes to a Guest in the house, and the Guest makes itself known. But the Guest does not intend to remain a Guest. Love comes to stay. Grace is God's self-gift to the human with the specific purpose of establishing a permanent *relationship*.

On the part of the Divine, this self-giving is of the very nature of God, the Truth that loves. Like a beggar standing with hat in hand, the Divine knocks, clears its throat, and waits. On the part of the human this approach looks for an *openness*, a space with the ache of longing. Before human awareness awakens, grace is one sided; Love is there merely as creative source. Once the human becomes aware, there is the invitation to open one's soul to Another, to Someone beyond the self. There is the tenuous opportunity for relationship. The Divine has come courting, begging entry (see Rev 3:20). The human consciousness looks up in the simple act of awareness. Then the soul turns and tentatively opens toward the Guest—or not. If we stay with the delicacy of this movement, we will be aware of how intricate the grace-human interplay is even at this early stage. The age-old question "Is this God's activity or human activity?" can only be answered with *yes*. Yes, the activity is initiated by God and empowered by God, and yes, the human is freely responding. If the human soul, enticed by the knock, turns and opens, the human accepts an encounter, grace enters awareness, and religious conversion begins. But what we must not miss is the fact that the dynamic is deeply *relational* like a dance. In watching dance partners, it is more accurate to say *they* are dancing,

---

[6] For a remarkable account of this experience, see Dag Hammarskjöld's *Markings* (New York: Knopf, 1965). This diary recounts Hammarskjöld's articulation of the movement of Mystery in his life and its effects through a largely secular lens.

not *he or she* is dancing. What we see is not just the motion of one of the dancers but the *relation* of the movements of each in response to the other, for what is happening is the *relation* of the movements of each in response to the other, not just one or the other.

The common Christian expression for the result of this initial encounter of the Divine and the human is "indwelling" (see John 14:23). Because of its relational delicacy, this triune gracing has usually been described as the indwelling of the Holy Spirit, that dynamic self-giving love of the Godhead. The sacramental symbol of this divine-human interface is usually oil, sweet-smelling chrism. Fire, blood, wind, wine, and water are also vibrant symbols of this reality. If the corner of a tissue is dipped into olive oil, we can watch with wonder as the oil permeates the tissue—saturating it completely as it climbs, yet in no way violating the tissue. The tissue remains a tissue, yet it will never be the same. The oil remains the oil, yet it now indwells the tissue, penetrating and bonding with it in a relationship of total fusion. Still, profound as this union is, the image limps. The God of the Christian tradition seeks more; this God seeks intimacy—the intimacy of a *friendship* (see John 15:15). In this Mutt and Jeff situation, the Divine now must transform the human in such a way that the human can commune with the Divine without being destroyed. To some extent, the human must be divinized for this friendship to even have a chance. Without this transformation, the human would be destroyed upon the approach of God.

Theological Virtue

The triune Mystery comes bearing gifts. The divine presence in the human must accommodate to the confines of human limitation. This accommodation by grace is a remarkable indication of the utter humbleness of God. The delicacy, the respect for the creature in its encounter with the Divine, is captured scripturally in the image of God protecting Moses with his hand as he passes by in Exodus 34:23. The encounter in itself, the gracious presence of the Divine, changes the very substance of the soul. Before, it was merely itself, sustained by the creative presence of God. Now it is indwelt and holds the Mystery of the Divine, which delicately accommodates itself to human fragility, disturbing nothing but enhancing everything.

What does this accommodation mean? The "customizing" of the Divine in the human is the marvel of what we have come to call "theological life" or "theological virtue" in the soul. These powers, I am going to suggest, make the human a new creature, capable of doing what it could not do before.[7]

The theological virtues are faith, hope, and charity. I am going to propose that they are triadic as is the Mystery itself and that they are designed to deify the human.[8] The human is taught, under the tutelage of this threefold influence, to *dance divinely*. The human is actually given a *created* equal footing for relationship with the Divine in these three powers.

The indwelling God is an incomprehensible Mystery. That deep Mystery, known only through the Son or Word, reorients the very *desire* of the human creature. From the depths of the undertow of its psychic energy, the human now *longs for nothing less than God*, for communion with this Mystery. This longing, born from the grasp of divine Love in the depths of its being, is the theological virtue of hope. It reorients the very passionate desire of the human creature. But true to its nature as a virtue or power for activity, hoping will manifest itself at the fourth level of consciousness in behavior that reveals religious orientation to the Divine in the fabric of our life. Hope does not know that for which it hopes, for it is the contribution of that hidden "Abba," or what we have named as "Father." This deep hidden nature of God is known only in and through the Word.

The Word is the very expression of this hidden Mystery. By the Word all that is comes to be (John 1:3). So it is by this Word that we come to *know* anything about this Mystery. It is the Word's presence that brings the human creature a new way of knowing. The theological virtue of faith is a *type of knowing* born of divine Love.[9] Born of the Love that has grasped the creature, faith reorients the entire human intelligence and its desire to know, to stop at nothing short of the Divine. The knowing has a new object. Mere human faith seeks human credibility. The

---

[7] In *Insight: A Study of Human Understanding* (Toronto: University of Toronto Press, 1992 [1957]), 696, 723, Lonergan refers to the theological virtues as "conjugate forms." My understanding of what he means is that as forms the theological virtues reorient the human toward acts that are now "under the influence" of the Divine and have a divine object. The human is given a new capability it would not have without them.

[8] Helminiak in *Religion and the Human Sciences: An Approach via Spirituality* (New York: SUNY, 1998) is careful to clarify what the term "deification" means (see 124–32). The term refers to human participation in divinity, not the making of the human into God.

[9] See Lonergan's *Method in Theology* (London: Darton, Longman and Todd, 1971), 115–19, for a careful distinction between faith and belief.

theological virtue, the direct gift of the self-expressive Word of God, permeates the consciousness and orients its knowing to the Divine. Theological faith wants to know more about who the Mystery is that has entered our life's horizon, where it comes from, and what it asks. While seeing in a glass darkly, faith enlists the intelligence to give it momentum. Reason, like a tiny child scooped up in an embrace after school, tries desperately to get its little arms around the Mystery, only too aware it will come up short. This means that faith will demand the careful questioning needed to reach *understanding*, and this will be followed by the careful reflection needed to reach a judgment of *what is so* about this Mystery. Faith permeates the cognitive operations, but as a virtue it is, like hope, a power to *act*. Like hope, faith will manifest itself in human choice. Decision on the fourth level of consciousness will reveal religious faith or its absence. Faith is a *decision* arising from a judgment of value that even though I may not fully know this Mystery, *I know I must cling to it*. The engagement of the intelligent operations follows, seeking ever to understand more. We might say that the healing vector through this virtue reorients the human intelligence to rest in nothing short of the Divine through a judgment of value, a judgment of primary worth.

As theological hope is longing born of divine Love[10] and theological faith is a knowing born of the Love that has grasped us, these facets of the triadic gift of grace in no way dispose of what is human or replace it. Rather, theological virtue enhances the human, making it capable of responding to the Divine with a created form of equality provided by God. Theological life frees the human from being confined to rational knowing alone. It opens the intelligence to the Divine itself as an object of knowing. Faith gives *substance* to the human longing transformed by hope. As faith aims at the very substance of our longing, God, so hope permeates our psychic energy in its desire and makes us ache for the Divine with inexpressible groanings (see Rom 8:26-27). We know not what we long for. Faith reveals the substance of that longing.

Like a blind person reading Braille, we have been feeling out the evidence of the divine presence in human consciousness, and we find ourselves changed, reoriented. In the midst of and flowing from the

---

[10] Tad Dunne has done careful work on this virtue, picking up some of what Lonergan left unfinished. See "Faith, Charity, and Hope," *Lonergan Workshop* 5 (1985): 49–70; and "Mystery," "Faith," and "Hope," in *Lonergan and Spirituality: Towards a Spiritual Integration* (Chicago: Loyola University Press, 1985), 116–26.

longing growing in us because of the presence of hidden Mystery, and the knowing that comes from Love, there is *the loving itself.* The Spirit is best expressed as a participle. There is the Love, the Beloved, and the Loving. Theological charity is *action* born of divine Love, action flowing from the fact that I have been loved first, and so I find myself "chariting." Born of the Love that has grasped us, loving actions become the offspring of this union. Our human loves would have us pursue what will satisfy us for a time. This loving is born of the Truth that loves and empowers us to love its way, in the way of agape. Such loving does not count the cost. It can go beyond self-interest without denying it. As a special sign of the Spirit's presence, the *dynamis* of active, self-giving love catches up the frail human emotion of love and gives us a capacity that surprises even ourselves. Because the Holy Spirit's loving is agape, we learn what real charity is: not a giving of our excess but a giving of our very substance with the free abandon of full choice.

The sensitive psyche with its rich emotions and longing for intimacy, the intellectual levels with their probing for truth, and the level of choice and decision—the entire soul is caught up in the grasp of the Divine through theological virtue. Faith reorients the capacity to know, hope reorients the capacity to long, and charity reorients the capacity of the human to freely choose; these theological virtues are all housed in the body's frail temple. This is the human, properly "possessed." This is the house lived in. This is grace in its threefold prism of theological life. This is the human equipped and poised for conscious relationship with the Divine. Clothed in newness like a transformed Cinderella, the human creature steps into the dance. Heady with the wine of theological life, the human wears see-through slippers. These make clear that her feet must remain very much on the ground.

Conversion and Further Transformation

Now the dance begins. Whether it will be the fancy footwork of the flamenco or the slow ease of the waltz remains to be seen. The Divine has come to deify the human, and so the work must proceed. Step by step, choice by choice, judgment by judgment, question by question, the putrid infection of self-service and egoism must be dissolved. Like a dutiful nurse, the Spirit of God begins the fiery cauterization, the cooling flooding, and the pouring in of oil and wine into the deep infection of the soul (cf. Luke 10:34).

What is conversion? We have already referred to an *initial* turning of the soul toward the Divine, the openness it brings, and the transformation grace brings, opening up the possibility of human response. *Religious conversion* is the tentative, fragile first turning, the go-for-broke decision of the human to admit the Divine into its life. One intends it, however cautiously. All of the conversions will be choices, for it is decision at the fourth level of consciousness that involves the human in the ongoing transformation that is the divine agenda. The initial change brought about here is the first step in a healing that will result in more and more transformation. The goal is to teach the human to dance divinely in all its operations. The means is progressive deification no matter the cost. Religious conversion, even if it is not known as such because the person experiencing it does not have the language, is the first of the conversions. As a result of it, we are religiously in love, whereas prior to it, we were not. We are different. We have a new reference point. The Divine has entered the field of our consciousness and will not go away. We might spend years after an initial religious experience burying its memory under the debris of other choices, but in the quiet of our aloneness we will remember. Religious conversion reorients one's life, but it is fragile. Once admitted, this Mystery may be relegated to the attic or the cellar of our lives in a desperate attempt to keep a little of ourselves for ourselves. But we know it all has to go. We need to sell it all. It takes time to learn, to our surprise, that all will be returned to us, and we find ourselves dealing properly with it for the first time. Religious conversion is but the beginning of further conversion—not an end.

Religious conversion takes different forms. The form it takes will depend on the tradition of the person who has had a religious experience. It takes a distinct Jewish, Islamic, or Buddhist form, and when a Christian experiences religious conversion it will take the form of Christian religious conversion. For the Christian, the Divine comes to meet us in the person of Christ Jesus. The incarnation becomes the bridge linking the Divine in the person of the Word to our humanness. In the bridge of the sacred humanity we come face-to-face with our own humanness and with the Divine, who has taken that humanness to itself in the human Jesus. The incarnation is the mirror image of our own limitation and transcendent tension. In the human Jesus we find our limitations, and in his divinity we find our own yearning for transcendence. Even more, we find in his humanity the same permeation by the Divine that we experience by grace in indwelling. We find the same human functioning in him that we are identifying in ourselves: an organism, psyche, and human spirit, a body and a soul assumed by the divine Word with no mixture or violation. For the Christian, self-knowledge in relation to the Divine at work in us is the heart of the process of transformation.

Often the first conversion to follow upon religious conversion, if we are approaching conversion with some hope of understanding time sequence, is *moral* conversion. It is a *change of behavior*. Because this has happened, I can no longer do thus and so. I can no longer do this or that. Because I have experienced this, I know I need to . . . We can recall Tommy and his mom's question. Falling in love with what's-her-name has prompted Tommy to clean himself up without being told for a change. His behavior has changed. He has sold his short-term satisfaction of lounging around in his sweats as long as possible to buy the possible admiring glances of his newfound love and the long-term good such a relationship might provide. This is the indicator of moral conversion. Short-term satisfaction is exchanged for long-term good. There are new priorities. Developing moral fiber might be the goal of self-discipline, and protecting the civil rights of citizens is hopefully the reason for law, but neither can produce the moral change that falling in love can bring about. The effects are remarkable. Effortlessly, all must be directed now to what I love. When what I have come to love is the divine Mystery, my life can be changed in ways others not in love as I am cannot understand.

Psychic conversion can be a traumatic experience. It involves psychic healing, the healing of memories, and forgiveness. We discussed dramatic bias earlier as a type of psychic scarring or scotosis. It is experienced as a type of unconscious censorship of the images that trigger memory of psychic pain or trauma. The psychic energy gets blocked or frozen. Psychic conversion is the dissolving of the censorship, and it can be experienced as a type of emotional release. This conversion is brought about by the intense experience of the accepting love of another or of the deep love of God in contemplative prayer. It also can be brought about through skillful therapy where the unconscious censorship is faced and intentionally dismantled with the help of a good therapist.

Intellectual conversion is the final type of conversion we will consider. Rare and infrequent, it is not the mere exchange of intellectual constructs. As understood by those who do intentionality analysis, it means *knowing how I come to know* and how that coming to know leads to my decisions. It means *self-appropriation of my own conscious operations* and being quite intentional about them. Intellectual conversion means knowing my own soul quite well and being about the business of deliberate soul building. Intellectual conversion is about the recognition of the biases in me and the honesty it will take to uproot them. My own individual, group, and general bias can often be revealed only through my contacts with others. I will notice them lurking beneath my anxieties, or someone else will point them out. Setting about the task of becoming more aware of one's own conscious operations can be quite a formidable task. To enter upon it will mean feeling the power of the creative vector at work. The creative vector moves relentlessly toward self-transcending transformation, from the keen observation of my experience, through my honest inquiry, to a tentative judgment of fact, and finally to a responsible judgment of value and a decision. It is time to consider what will give *evidence* that the transformation is indeed coming about.

Cardinal Moral Virtue

The healing brought about by religious, Christian, moral, and psychic conversion is all for the creating that will come about by power of the virtues we call "cardinal" or "moral." Far from being some kind of moral straightjacket, virtue is the capacity and strength to act consistently toward the good. No mindless habits, these virtues enable human choice to stay on course without having to negotiate every choice anew. If the person is intellectually converted and is familiar with intentionality analysis, he or she can be quite attentive to the demands of the creative vector. The person can then enter into the creative unfolding of his or her own humanness with conscious awareness and intent. All of the above—the conversions, the dissolving of bias, the freeing of human potential by the healing vector, and the actualization of that potential under the impetus of the creative vector—have one goal: the human transformation toward deification.

What is this transformation? What is the human to be? Scripture makes it clear that we know not what we shall be but that grace indeed is at work in us. The Divine that grasps us has but one intent: to unite us with itself. To effect this union, a process of *theosis* must go on, a term given to this transformation by Eastern Christians.[11] All that is broken in the human needs to be healed. All that is sinful must be

---

[11] See Helminiak, *Religion and the Human Sciences*, 123–58, for a development of theosis from a psychological perspective. For a more theological explanation from an Eastern point of view, see Vladimir Lossky, *The Mystical Theology of the Eastern Church*

purified. Union with the living God allows for no dross remaining on the gold. We can state *that* this is so and *that* this process is a vital part of the destiny of the human being, but we need to press on to *how* it might actually take place. What do we watch for to know the human is being transformed? Is there empirical evidence?

Theological virtue is subtle. Spiritual directors are attuned to the sound of someone faithing, hoping, and chariting. The rest of us need to be clued in to what to watch for. We do not ordinarily use participles for the theological virtues, but doing so stresses the dynamic and operative nature of the change in one who is responding to religious experience. The three theological virtues in a human being give that person the power for godly activity. Such persons know God through faith. They long for this Mystery in hope, and they already possess what they long for to the extent that their humanness can bond with the Divine in active charity. The source is God, the virtue is God's gracious gift, and the increase in faith, hope, and charity is God's doing. We ask, and we receive.

But there are two involved in this dance. Wallflower though the human may be, once the Divine says, "May I have this dance?" and leads the hesitant human out on the floor, there is *human* work to do, human steps to take. Swept along under the lead of theological life, what's a human to do? The Divine wants no shotgun weddings. The human needs to enter the dance in full, free human response. We have already referred to the healing vector as a cauterizing energy pull in the human to dissolve sin and its effect, bias. The evidence of actual *healed human activity* is what we in the Christian tradition call "moral virtue."

The four cardinal moral virtues originate in the Jewish wisdom tradition (see Wis 8:6-7) and from the wisdom tradition of the Greeks. Aristotle identified *prudence, justice, fortitude,* and *temperance* as the hallmarks of the heroic human being. Thomas Aquinas agreed, and these four powers in the person became evidence of spiritual development for Christians as well.[12] Reference to religious experience or conversion aside, society holds up citizens who are prudent, just, and brave and whose lives show moderation. Mainline culture offers wise, just, brave, and balanced persons as models for its citizens, particularly its youth. So the human, depending on upbringing, education, and

---

(Crestwood, NY: St. Vladimir's Seminary Press, 1976), 196–216; and *In the Image and Likeness of God* (Crestwood, NY: St. Vladimir's Seminary Press, 1985), 97–110.

[12] See Thomas Aquinas, *Summa Theologiae*, II-II, beginning with q. 47.

training, can start the growth of these powers or habits in day-to-day living. But should the Mystery of the Divine enter the person's horizon, Thomas tells us God comes bearing gifts of not three, but seven virtues. The divine union brought about by charity in the human consciousness becomes like a Midas touch. These virtues become ways of living out that loving. No longer merely nice ways to be human, they become part of the theosis, of the godliness in the making. When the Divine is part of the human's horizon, charity (God's way of loving) acts as the *form* of each of the moral virtues.[13]

Rather than just tipping our hats and going on, it would do us well to probe what this might mean. To begin, the acknowledgment that active divine love is the very form of these virtues might refocus our understanding of them as *infused* and *acquired*. Since charity is their form, they are infused as potential human responses now actually shaped by charity, God's own compassionate way of loving. They become acquired as the person engages in activity that develops them. Furthermore, charity will demand their development. To allow these capabilities to remain dormant in one's behavior is not merely an unfortunate neglect. It is an insult to charity.

Love's Discretion: Prudence

Prudence is love's discretion. It assists the creative vector in calling for keen attentiveness on the experiential level, careful questioning on the second level of consciousness, and wise reflection before coming down in the third level in judgment as to the truth of the facts. Unlike the theological virtues, of which there can never be too much, the moral virtues become more perfect the more they stick to a *mean* determined by human reason. Not too much, not too little. Too little prudence makes one dangerous. Too much makes one into an overly cautious prude who will never risk new human effort. As we might expect, because prudence strengthens the creative vector as it works with the intellectual operations of levels 2 and 3, this virtue is the guide for justice, fortitude, and temperance. The creative vector urges the consciousness to continually heighten its operations from level to

---

[13] Sources that are more current on Thomas's virtue theory include Jean Porter, *The Recovery of Virtue: The Relevance of Aquinas for Christian Ethics* (Louisville, KY: Westminster/John Knox, 1990); and Paul Wadell, *The Primacy of Love: An Introduction to the Ethics of Thomas Aquinas* (New York/Mahwah: Paulist, 1992).

level as the human is freed from the bondage of bias. But we need to remember that these virtues, both theological and moral, will all be *manifest* at the fourth level of consciousness. They are choices on how to act humanly under the influence of grace, and they will play out in daily existential decisions. The piloting or guiding of the other virtues by prudence is hinted at in its three principle stages: taking counsel, forming a judgment, and commanding execution. Thomas explored these practical realities long before Lonergan thematized them by introducing us to intentionality analysis.

Love's Fairness: Justice

Justice is love's fairness. For our purpose here we need to know that justice directs our choices in our relations with others, including the Divine. It is a perpetual or continuing intent to render to each what is that one's due. It directly concerns operations of choice and so, with the guidance offered by prudence, strengthens the creative vector in its urge to be responsible at the fourth level of consciousness. Justice is of two kinds: *commutative*, which assesses relations between two persons, and *distributive*, which assesses relations between a person and a community. It is not difficult to understand the direct connection of this virtue with the dissolving of individual, group, and general bias. All three of these biases will dismiss the right of another individual or group to be heard and respected.

Love's Courage: Fortitude

Fortitude is love's strength. It deals with the obstacles and hindrances to prudence and justice. These hindrances can come in the form of indulgence or the revulsion that comes from the oppressive difficulty of decisions I need to make. General fortitude is simply a steadfastness of mind. Special fortitude undertakes dangerous action or endures painful toil after sufficient reflection. In either case, fortitude deals with fear and daring in the face of obstacles. Its first act is plain endurance. Then it plunges in. Fortitude uses anger for its energy. Fear distorts the mean on the side of inaction, and fearlessness tips it in the direction of foolishness. It is not hard to see the guiding role of prudence in fortitude. What is little understood today is the outcome of a courageous act in the consciousness. It brings about a *delight that is an antidote to depression*. From the above it is clear why I am going to suggest that this power is given as an aid to the emotional energy of the psyche, specifically to the more considered (irascible) emotions of fear, courage, hope, despair, and anger. As with all virtue, fortitude will manifest itself on the fourth level of consciousness through action or patient and prudent inaction.

Love's Moderation: Temperance

Temperance is love's moderation. Rather than acting the part of a finger-wagging chaperone, temperance calls for a true celebration of the body. It is a "tempering" through intelligence, and it puts no restraint on pleasure that corresponds to intelligence. Thomas insists that un-addressed pleasure and a neglect of proper nourishment of the senses through beauty results in promiscuity. This insight could make a difference in something as simple as rehabbing a seedy neighborhood with a high crime rate. Temperance, with prudence's strong hand, dismisses restriction imposed by custom when it's clear that practical wisdom knows what is needed. Temperance restrains our tendency toward attraction, just as fortitude nerves us to deal with threats. Its mark is tranquility of mind and a sense of beauty, understood by Thomas as a sense of measured proportion or balance. Under the guidance of prudence, temperance governs the animal dimensions of human life, restraining their capacity to debase the human while simultaneously celebrating the human capacity for bodily pleasure. Fear of sensual pleasure distorts the mean of temperance, as does self-indulgence. An interesting insight that could be invaluable to the modern struggle for the appropriate use of sexual energy is Thomas's conviction that cour-age at times must demand the *increase* of a passion in order for it to "burn off" self-gratification. An example of this might be suggesting to teens highly infatuated and filled with sexual desire to love and long for the beloved so intensely that no action be requested that might result in harm to the other. This introduces the element of self-sacrifice (in this case in the form of temperance), which is exactly what is needed for mature love to move beyond infatuation.[14]

Contrary to the popular notion of the role of temperance in moder-ating drink and food intake, temperance is directed primarily to "skin hunger." Rather than regulating food or drink, temperance is about

---

[14] For a fuller discussion of this dynamic, see Thomas J. Tyrrell, *Urgent Longings: Reflections on Infatuation, Intimacy, and Sublime Love* (Mystic, CT: Twenty-Third Publications, 1994).

regulating the human need for touch. It is really concerned not with pleasure as such but primarily with pleasure as it pertains to touch. It is concerned with pleasures that preserve the individual, with coupling between male and female for reproduction of the human species, and finally with food and drink, because they too preserve the well-being of the individual. Much is being written today on the importance of the need for touch as the basis of physical and psychological health. A careful tending to nourishing skin hunger in childhood and filling the senses with beauty might go a long way toward healing a sexually promiscuous society.

The power of temperance in the soul unleashes a healthy shame-facedness that recoils from bodily debasement. It reveals an honesty that delights in the beauty of the balance that temperance brings. It will suggest abstinence and sobriety when appropriate. In regard to procreation, it will offer chastity, which guides the appropriateness of intercourse itself, and purity, which governs the movements and touches that accompany intercourse. It is purity, then, that regulates what will or will not be done in sexual foreplay and so-called kinky sex. Modesty, another assistant to temperance, deals with dress, the signals given to attract another, bodily movements, and all that pertains to the beauty of the human being in its bodiliness. It doesn't miss a trick: walking, glances, hand gestures, posturing. Temperance orchestrates and cho-reographs our bodily presence in the world under the baton of love.

The direct evidence of temperance will again be manifest at the fourth level of consciousness: existential behavior; choices; decisions; action or the restraint of action. It is also clear from the description above that along with fortitude this virtue has immediate effect on the psychic energy of the person. Temperance regulates what we have called the more spontaneous (concupiscible) emotions. Fortitude under prudence's guidance moderates fear, and temperance under that same discretion moderates desire. Nothing is left unaided. The psyche in its dynamic energy has two cardinal virtues to assist in its transformation.

The human spirit in its operations of intelligence and free choice is given the power in prudence and justice to open up the possibil-ity of what being fully human really means. The body becomes the means of communication for that full humanness. These four virtues of prudence, justice, fortitude, and temperance get the human out on the cosmic dance floor on its own two legs. Held in the arms of Love, which has grasped it in the totality of its humanness, it moves. The Love that holds it knows the human dance and has come to meet it on its own terms, on equal footing. Flowing from grace, these powers are indeed given. They are infused with charity. But the moral virtues would remain sterile if the human chooses not to develop them. Engaging these powers in freedom, we acquire the sureness and flow of their operation in consciousness, and they reveal themselves in our daily decisions.

The new creation comes as a threefold gift from the Love that has caught the attention of the human consciousness. Faith transforms the operations of intelligence, hope transforms human desire, and charity transforms the acts that flow from both. The human is reoriented to the Divine. In grasping the human to itself in loving union, however fragile, the Divine causes the human to be immediately generative. The human begins to heal from the toxicity of egoism under the influence of *gratia sanans*, the grace called "sanctifying" or "healing," a dynamic we have described as the healing vector. With each release from bias and with each inch-by-inch ongoing conversion, the creative vector *actualizes* grace (now called "actual grace") to transform broken humanness into human beauty. The goal of prudence, justice, fortitude, and temperance is not God in this life. The goal is the full flourishing of the human and its regeneration and transformation.

Gifts of the Holy Spirit

God comes not only as Guest bearing gifts. God owns the property, takes up residence, dons an apron, and keeps house. Through the moral virtues the master of the house is very much in charge and fully engages us in its remodeling. There is a very important facet to consider, however, as part of the divine foundation. The healing and creative transformation of the human in its total being is going to need all the outside help it can get. Without the help of the Divine, we can do nothing, whether we admit it or not.

The presence of the Divine in the depths of the human is itself a formidable gift. This is no generator stored away in a room in the basement. The presence of the Divine is an anointing, a fragrance that fills every room. By the presence of the active love of the Spirit, the transformation of the human through the virtues, both theological and moral, is assisted actively by this very presence. The gifts of the Holy Spirit are not virtues. They are not powers given so that the person can make a truly *human* response. They are direct helps from the Divine to the entire transformative process. They come with that Divine presence and are felt often as a surprise, a *being carried* in the face of real human limits. The scriptural basis for the Christian reference to the gifts of the Holy Spirit can be found in Isaiah 11, but the reference is no proof text. The text gives us a scriptural base for an understanding of God's activity in our lives. The classical listing of the seven gifts of the Spirit is the church's way of pointing to a *fullness of Divine presence*, flooding the human with mercy for every need. Said another way, the gifts are not merely occasional help from God. Their function is evidence of God's very presence within the human being. Their source is God in the person of the Holy Spirit. When they function the human *shines*.

In Cognitive Operation: Wisdom, Understanding, and Knowledge

The cognitive operations move with ease under *wisdom's* influence. This gift dilates the human horizon, relating scattered data from life's experience, understanding, and judgments into an integrated whole. In the context of faith and love, wisdom, like a compass, sets the intelligence in the direction to which hope points. *Understanding* as a gift of the Spirit does not depend on scholarly effort. It is a gift for mystagogy—the grasping of the meaning of Scripture and liturgy as it relates to contemporary life. *Knowledge* is the intimate knowing of one's place in the created universe. It is a knowing of oneself as a part of, not over and above and against, the sun and moon and stars and all the creatures of the earth. It is the gift of "knowing my place" amid all God's creation and being delighted with the truth of it.

In Evaluative/Decisional Operation: Counsel and Piety

The evaluative operations leading to decision also get help. *Counsel* draws its data from both judgments of fact and judgments of value—not only my own but those of others I find credible. Thomas suggests that counsel assists the virtue of prudence. This might mean that counsel prods the intelligence to attend to all of prudence's steps of deliberation. All is finally brought before the bar of Love for arbitration. The decision, as a result, may come out looking different to the casual observer. Usual cultural values may not carry the day. *Piety* often gets falsely represented. Rather than hands-folded pietism, the gift is a gut sense of reverence. It brings the person the ability to detect the burning bush in the strangest terrain, with the result that the shoes of the soul go off and we are caught up in awe. Piety gives us a nose for the hidden sacred. We spot it, or rather it grasps us. Thomas suggests that the gift of piety especially helps the virtue of justice, giving God and others the reverence they are due.

In Spontaneous and Considered Emotion:
Fear of the Lord and Fortitude

Psychic energy and its emotions are not overlooked. The pleasure seeking of the spontaneous emotions are fine-tuned by a loving *fear.* Fear of the Lord brings my loves and longings before Love's bar. With Love's hand on the rudder, this holy fear would have these motors run without guilt and shame in joy. The considered fight-or-flight emotions, developed with guidance from the virtue of fortitude, are assisted by the gift of *fortitude.* Like a shot of divine adrenaline, this gift often makes itself known in a crisis. When all is said and done, this gift may be behind the spontaneous acts of self-giving heroism of ordinary people who have not been known to be brave at all in the ebb and flow of ordinary life. They are surprised at themselves and know that they were "carried" by God through a tough situation.

We have been considering the divine foundations of spirituality: grace, indwelling, theological virtue, conversion, moral virtue, and the gifts of the Holy Spirit. A sound Christian spirituality will grow from an interface of the human and the Divine. The goal of spiritual growth from a Christian perspective is the transformation of the human in and by its intimate union with the Divine. How will we know this transformation has happened? What is it that we are looking for? How will we recognize the evidence when we see it? It is to the *results* that we now turn, for the tree will be known by its fruits.

Summary

1. The Divine encounters the human in the context of its very humanness. The being of each person is *worded* into existence in the Word, establishing the basic relation of creature to Creator. Grace or "favor" is present, on God's part, from the very beginning of the person's life. Present also is the woundedness passed on to all of us by the accumulated decisions made by our ancestors. In each of us is the inherited history of the human rejection of the Mystery we call God, woven into our human DNA. This rejection, called "original sin" among Christians, is experienced as the shame of being a limited creature. Fury at the fact that we are not God but our limited, humble selves often

results in violence toward ourselves and others. When the Divine makes its presence known in consciousness and the human opens toward it, the dis-ease has already begun to lose its grip. *Religious experience* is a most radical summons to turn toward Another. The arrogance of sin loses its grip, allowing the initial intended relationship to be restored. Grace is now experienced in the consciousness as being grasped by divine Love, and it dawns on me that it's OK for me to be my limited, humble self. Love long present in the depths of my being now emerges in my awareness. The hidden recesses, the height or depth of the soul, and the psychospiritual dimension of the human where this drama is experienced are what we have referred to as the *apex animae*.

2. With the human now open, the triune Mystery begins to permeate the consciousness. This permeation effects a transformation in the very capacities of human operation through the *theological virtues*. Desire in the human expands to a longing that will be satisfied now with nothing less than God. This longing for the Holy is the theological virtue of hope. The cognitive operations of the intelligence now seek to know this Mystery, and faith gives the human the capacity to know God, although in a glass darkly. The evaluative operations that will lead to decision now consider the Mystery among its values. The presence of this Love prompts loving acts through the theological virtue of charity. Faith, hope, and charity, capacities born from divine Love, are now at home in the human. Hope is the gift of the hidden Father, faith is bestowed by the Word, and active love flows from the Spirit. The human is now *indwelt* and aware of a presence of Mystery. Its operative capacities have been transformed. The human can now act godly.

3. *Religious conversion*, if firm, creates a state of being in love with divine Mystery. Religious conversion is Christian when the experience of Mystery comes in the person of Christ Jesus. This first of the conversions opens the way for *moral conversion*, a new preference for long-term good over short-term satisfaction in the choices one makes. Religious conversion also ushers in the deep love that can effect *psychic conversion*: the dissolving of the psychic censorship of images that trigger past trauma. *Intellectual conversion* may follow if the person has made the turn to intentionality analysis. This conversion makes the person privy to the operations of his or her own consciousness. The person becomes capable of monitoring his or her own functions, thus becoming an active participant in one's soul making.

4. Theological virtue transforms the human, giving it godly capacities. Now the *cardinal moral virtues* reorient human behavior. The

Love that has grasped the human through religious conversion has but one goal: the total union of the human with itself. The theological virtue of charity is now the *form* shaping the human response to this divine initiative. The powers infused into human consciousness to re-shape the human are the cardinal moral virtues. Unlike the theological virtues, which originate in the Mystery, the moral virtues are infused as potentialities and remain sterile without human engagement. Prudence, justice, fortitude, and temperance will shrivel without human activity. Because charity is the form of these moral virtues, prudence can be described as love's discretion, justice is love's fairness, fortitude is love's courage, and temperance is love's moderation. At their core is very human activity: the operations of intelligence, choice, and the psychic energy of emotion.

5. The presence of Love in the human brings the power of seven major virtues to engage the person in active response. Love also makes its presence known directly by what have been called the *gifts of the Holy Spirit*. These gifts, active from the divine presence of the Holy Spirit of God, act like an anointing of the human from within. These gifts assist the human in its response to both theological and moral virtues. The Spirit's presence is like an inner radiance. The classical listing names seven, drawn from Isaiah 11, but the number is largely symbolic. Wisdom, understanding, knowledge, counsel, piety, fortitude, and fear of the Lord are but major indications of the untold intricate and delicate ways in which the human is influenced by the Spirit of God in its midst. The classical listing, upon a closer look, applies to this influence in cognitive operations, in decision making, and in both spontaneous and considered emotions.

CHAPTER SIX

The Beautiful Human Being

Naming the Beauty: In the Human

Her face glowed. She sat in her wheelchair, her wispy white hair framing her usual smile, and repeated over and over, "Would you believe it, I'm ninety-three today! Isn't that a marvel? I've been around ninety-three years!" "Beauty" is a rather rare word in a systematic study about spiritual development. The usual description of the spiritual person will center on prayer or moral integrity. Yet what captures us again and again is beauty—the beauty of the fireworks, of the sunset, of someone's eyes, of some artwork. Most of all, what moves us is the beauty of someone's life. This is the stuff of the good novel—a story of a life that thrills us. But beauty is also the stuff of good spirituality, and the results we are considering in this chapter are first of all beautiful.

What is beauty?[1] Defined by some as the merging of truth and goodness in a way that is available to the senses, we will use the word to describe authentic humanness, the comeliness of the physical, the unblocked flow of psychic energy, and the unbiased and free operations of the human spirit. This full flowering is the agenda of grace, and it includes the transformation of the human that we call "deification." This transformation means the gradual preparation of the human for risen life.

In this chapter we will consider the evidence of this transformation in progress. In the Christian tradition the common way to refer to this evidence is with the term given us in Scripture: "fruits." The fruits of the Holy Spirit will give evidence of the work of the Divine in a human

---

[1] For a deep treatment of the theme of beauty as it applies to spirituality, see John O'Donohue, *Beauty: The Invisible Embrace* (New York: HarperCollins, 2004).

life. A second bit of evidence is in the human capacity for forgiveness. But perhaps the clearest evidence of all is the blessedness or beatitude, the "happiness" of those whose lives exude a tone, a steady state of beauty that gives meaning to the expression "beautiful people." The Beatitudes at face value do not refer to a beauty that can be perceived with the eye. The translations use the terms "blessed" or "happy." I am choosing to use the term "beautiful" not to negate the usual translation but to expand it. Blessedness or happiness is a human *condition*. That the human condition is changed by the action of grace has hopefully been shown. But the term "beauty" makes this graced condition *observable* in some way. In some way the senses perceive it. The beauty we encounter may be more sensed than seen. Mother Teresa was elderly and frail physically. But she was very beautiful as a person. It is this radiance that we are trying to acknowledge. Finally, we will consider the key means of nourishing the beauty already present, the vital role of prayer in the life of the Christian in the world.

We have explored the fact that when Love comes calling, it bears gifts. We have seen that theological life in terms of faith, hope, and charity transforms the human, making it capable of godly activity. But this godly activity is *human*, and the moral virtues, powers also freely given, have as their purpose the full activation of all that is human. Where is all this leading?

It is clear from the evening news that the human, broken and wounded by generations of egotistical decisions on the part of our forebears, is prone to ugly behavior. Yet when grasped by Love, this same human becomes radiant, a being capable of remarkable beauty. To understand the mystery of this wooing for restoration, Christians return to what has been shown them in the wisdom traditions of their Scriptures. The Jewish texts of the First Testament, especially the Song of Solomon, reveal the Divine as hotly in pursuit of the human. Rejected, the Divine waits like some wounded lover for the human to cease its whoring. The divine image, imprinted in the being of the human, repeatedly becomes distorted, disfigured, and disabled. The hidden depths of the psyche, a rich seedbed of emotion, images, and dreams, can suffer from the amnesia of being cut off from any memory of its source. The result is an emotional life fraught with restlessness and anxiety. The intelligence, capable of the marvel of insight, knowledge, and speech, can be locked in the prattle of its own egotistical self-talk. Its knowing can be confined to the contingent, to the sensory world. As a result, the glorious human capacity to choose freely will then make choices that serve no more than its own needs. The Divine, whose triadic image in the human has been rejected, responds with a passionate extravagance. This Lover says, "You have destroyed my image in you, so I will take on *your* image to restore it. I will bring you home to yourself and to myself not in spite of you but in partnership with you."

The Christian Scriptures are the revelation of the Divine come to seek us by taking on our humanness. This Second Testament shows us where this leads. The transfiguration of the human Jesus on Mount Tabor (Mark 9:2-8; Matt 17:1-8) so fixates the apostles with its beauty that they don't want to leave. Yet this experience is but a preview of the permanent transformation of the humanness of the risen Jesus. This transformed humanness will be "taken home" in the mystery of the ascension. For too long these two scriptural events have been viewed by Christians as wonderful things happening to *Jesus*. We have missed the point that what happens to his sacred humanity is what is in store for *us*.

Remarkably, the mangled, bruised, and bloody humanity of Jesus has been the focus of Christian reflection and prayer for centuries. Far from revolting or disgusting, the crucified Jesus draws the human heart like a magnet. As a revelation of intense self-giving love, the crucified ends up being something of radiant and breathtaking beauty. This remarkable beauty of Jesus coming into his own is the very glory of God.[2] Coming into our full humanness will likewise be the glory of God. It will be coming home. And it will be coming into a breathtaking beauty. Somehow, the very brokenness of the crucified allows the light of the Divine to stream into the world.

The frontispiece of this book holds the image of a tree rooted within a circle. The text, from *The Dialogue* of Catherine of Siena, will provide the metaphor for this final chapter. Our destiny is the full beauty of the human, a beauty that can be realized only in its intimate relationship

---

[2] In prayer 20 of Catherine of Siena we find this remarkable passage: "Now I know for certain that you spoke the truth when you appeared to your two disciples on the road as a traveler. You said that Christ had to suffer so, and by the way of the cross enter into his glory. . . . They failed to understand because their minds were darkened. But you understood yourself. What then was your glory, O gentle loving Word? You yourself—and you had to suffer in order to enter into your very self!" *The Prayers of Catherine of Siena*, trans. and ed. Suzanne Noffke, OP (New York: Paulist, 1983; 2nd ed., San Jose: Author's Choice Press, 2001).

with the Divine, not apart from it. This relationship is unfolding in the consciousness in a manner akin to the growth of a living organism, but far beyond it. Now that we have named it, what does this mean? What is this beauty that is our destiny? How do we recognize an authentic human being?

Knowing the Beauty: Fruits and Beatitudes

If beauty is understood as the fusion of truth and goodness, and if, in the Divine, truth, goodness, and beauty are all one, then we have an explanation of what we mean by "holiness." For those who follow Thomas, the beautiful is that which when seen gives great pleasure, thus assuring the inclusion of a full, rich sensuality in the delight beauty brings.[3] In the Divine, beauty is the summation of the very holiness of God. Human beauty, then, is the holiness that results from divine-human intimacy. It is a beauty that is not merely interior; it is able to be seen, to be felt, to be heard, to be touched. It is empirically observable. Based on a relationship of intimacy, holiness understood in terms of human beauty of body and soul can then be distinguished from religious experience, religious conversion, and the practices of religion. All of these are part of our lives, yet they fail to produce evidence of the holiness we are seeking to understand as human beauty.

The union realized in this intimacy is not for the self alone. The seeker journeys among other seekers. For the Christian there is the community of other Christians, as well as those given to us in special relationships. It is here that the beauty is to be first seen, felt, and celebrated. It is in the faith community that the union with the Divine becomes spiritually generative.[4] Once grasped by God, the human enters a deeper transforming process, completing the work the moral

---

[3] See Alejandro Garcia-Rivera, *The Community of the Beautiful: A Theological Aesthetics* (Collegeville, MN: Liturgical Press, 1999), and John Navone, *Enjoying God's Beauty* (Collegeville, MN: Liturgical Press, 1999). Drawing from a variety of sources, these authors develop the insights offered here to great length.

[4] In an image that speaks more profoundly than a multitude of words, Catherine of Siena makes a clear distinction between the tree's flower and fruit: "God wants from this tree only the flower of glory; the fruit he leaves for us. And when this tree is full-grown, it stretches out its branches and offers its fruit to its neighbors—in whatever way it can, honestly and with warm love." Letter T113, to Bandecca Salimbeni, in *The Letters of Catherine of Siena*, vol. 2, trans. Suzanne Noffke (Tempe, AZ: Arizona Center for Medieval and Renaissance Studies, 2001), 675.

virtues began from childhood. The direct action of the Holy Spirit comes to play in our lives in the most practical ways through gifts identified as wisdom, understanding, knowledge, counsel, fortitude, piety, and fear of the Lord.[5] The human then blossoms and begins to bear tangible fruit. This fruit is practical and nourishing. It can be felt, smelled, tasted, and enjoyed.

We return again to the frontispiece image of the tree. Planted in the circle that is divine Love, the tree's root, its love, lives only on Love. This root (its love) is planted firmly in the earth, the *humus* of self-knowledge joined to the circle. The tree is firmly planted. The consciousness is permeated with its life's Love through faith, hope, and charity, reorienting it to the Divine. Now able to function with God's own way of longing, knowing, and loving, it begins to function spiritually as permeated with Love. It develops humanly, extending itself by the practice of prudence, justice, fortitude, and temperance. The gifts of the Spirit act like Son-shine, energizing the sap, the very lifeblood of the tree. It is the Spirit's activity in the human that is the ultimate source of anything humanly beautiful showing up in the life. What is showing is truly human in its manifestation. The *dynamis* in the water, wine, blood, wind, fire, and oil (Spirit symbols) making this tree really live is this Spirit energy in its active, dynamic, self-giving power. The Spirit is the power in the "juice" entering the tree's root (its own love) giving life the tree could not give to itself, or of itself.

To be clear, this divine activity works in and through the human. The life energy of the human being works humanly. None of this human operation is replaced by the Divine. Human energy flows creatively from the heart of God. The life energy of the human being can choose good or ill. As human we activate the pure possibility that unfolds by decisions we make. Human consciousness opens or closes to the Divine, which seeks to influence those choices. Grace entices the consciousness to *open*, and once opened, the consciousness makes choices *under the influence* of the Divine. Like a drunkard who sees through the wine, speaks through the wine, and acts through the wine, the human under the influence of the Spirit of God sees, speaks, and acts under that Spirit's influence.[6] The consciousness makes its fourth-level

---

[5] Found in Isaiah 11:2-3—we again need to keep in mind that the gifts listed are not exhaustive.

[6] Catherine writes using the "opening" image: "In God's light we see light. In the warmth of God all our heart's chill and tepidity is burned up, if only we use our freedom

choices and makes them freely, in reality more freely than in its former closed condition. There is no replacement of the human by the Divine. Rather, the Divine empowers all that was disabled and distorted in the human. Like sunlight in a room or like the fragrance that fills the air by enhancing but not violating it, so does this Spirit's presence and power permeate the consciousness. What does this "fragrance," this "light," this "intoxication," effect in the human? How might we recognize the fruitfulness, the lift, the comfort of this fiery permeation of ourselves?

We find the fruits of the Holy Spirit in Paul's letter to the Galatians 5:22-23. The list names nine fruits, but tradition has expanded them to some of those named here: charity, joy, peace, patience, benignity (mildness, gentleness, goodness, or kindness), generosity, faithfulness, long-suffering (longanimity), and self-control (modesty, continence, and chastity).[7] Again, the exact number of fruits of the Spirit is not our concern. The numbers often indicate a fullness, a completeness, and so are more symbolic than definitive, as are the gifts of the Holy Spirit in Isaiah 11. In contrast to virtues and gifts, we need to know what these fruits mean. What *are* the fruits, and how do they differ from the virtues and the gifts?

The fruits indicate a type of productivity, a tangible evidence of the tree's life. We can experience fruitfulness. Fruit also points to nourishment, to something pleasing to the eye, to a firmness to the touch, and

---

of choice to open the window of our will so the sunlight can come into our soul's house." Letter T315, to Pietro da Milano, Carthusian, in *The Letters of Catherine of Siena*, vol. 4, trans. Suzanne Noffke (Tempe, AZ: Arizona Center for Medieval and Renaissance Studies, 2008), 94–95.

[7] The Dominicans, and in particular Reginald Garigou-Lagrange, OP, have carefully studied St. Thomas and made every effort to relate the virtues, gifts, fruits, and the Beatitudes in a systematic schema. As examples, see Reginald Garigou-Lagrange, OP, *Christian Perfection and Contemplation* (St. Louis: B. Herder Book Co., 1937), 296; Bede Jarrett, OP, *The Abiding Presence of the Holy Ghost in the Soul* (Westminster, MD: The Newman Bookshop, 1918); and Jerome Wilms, OP, *Divine Friendship according to St. Thomas* (London: Blackfriars Publications, 1958). This effort to understand the relationship of the elements in the divine-human encounter were, I believe, first attempts to explain the interaction of grace and human freedom at a time when interiority analysis was unknown and the categories of "ascetical" and "mystical" were used. For a more contemporary assessment of the value and clarity of Thomas's work on the virtues and gifts, see Dennis J. Billy, "Growing in the Virtues and the Gifts: Spiritual Direction as a Practical Theological Locus for the Convergence of Spirituality and Morality," *Studia Moralia* 39:2 (2001): 433–59.

to a delight for the sense of smell. We are being given an image of the results of a development, a maturing, a collaborative labor between the human and the Divine. The tree's flower holds a promise. The flower points to a glory still to come. The fruit is the realization of that promise. The *intent* of the human creature is a promise, and God receives glory by its very fact. God delights in both the intent and its gradual realization as the human comes into fruit or actualization. The fruit is nourishment for the neighbor. It ministerially feeds the community. Maturing in virtue under the influence of the Spirit of God makes human presence and action ministerial food for the men and women, the children and teens, the prisoners and homeless who come by—sweet fruit indeed.

The divine-human dance has been reasoned, charted, and analyzed in the earlier part of this study. The Christian community recounts it in various ways by various writers. But it is in the images of the mystics that we have an accuracy that supersedes logic's limits. Relational and flowing, the interaction we have reasonably named and pigeonholed laughs at us and skips on. The interaction of the Spirit in our spirit pours us out like a fountain; it entices, seduces, woos, and cauterizes us until we not only humanly taste good but give forth the fragrance of blessing. Charity, joy, peace, patience, and the rest are not abstract qualities. They are concrete fruits of a blessedness that is beautiful.

Being blessed, happy, or beautiful is being a certain kind of person. It is being a beatitude person (see Matt 5:3-11). The shorter list of the Beatitudes in Luke is amplified to eight in Matthew's gospel. Many have written on the Beatitudes. I suggest that they relate to the divine and human foundations as the *tone* or *fragrance of the total life* of a person whose consciousness is permeated with God, like a custom-composed song or a spiritual designer cologne.[8] The fruit is there. It

---

[8] In a beautiful passage in *The Dialogue*, God uses the image of sounding to describe the soul permeated by grace: "Oh, how they have harmonized their organs through that good gentle guard, free choice, who stands at the gate of the will! All their senses make one sweet sound, which comes forth from the center of the city of the soul because all her gates are both opened and closed. Her will is closed to selfishness and open to desire and love of my honor and affection for her neighbors. Her understanding is closed to the sight of the world's pleasures . . . but open and fixed with lightsomeness on the light of my Truth. Her memory is locked to sensual thoughts of the world and herself, but open to receive and remember my blessings. The soul's movements, then, make a jubilant sound, its chords tempered and harmonized with prudence and light, all of them melting into one sound, the glorification and praise of my name. Into this

can be seen, heard, and felt. The Beatitudes are presented in Scripture as coming directly from the mouth of Jesus. Rather than reflecting on them as the behavior of Christians beyond commandment morality, which is the common way they are taught, I suggest we ponder them as the revelation of Jesus' own mature spirituality. He is, in his humanity, beautiful. He is a blessing. What happens to our self-image when we read the Beatitudes in this way?

We usually read the Beatitudes beginning with the word "blessed" or "happy." What happens to the meaning if we use the term "beautiful"?

"Beautiful are the poor in spirit, for theirs is the kingdom of heaven." Thomas relates this beatitude to the Spirit's gift of fear. As a holy fear of dishonoring the Love that has grasped me, the gift of fear relates to the virtue of temperance, or Love's moderation. The tone of "poor in spirit" gives evidence of the humble truth that we have nothing we have not received (cf. 1 Cor 4:7). In the divine consciousness of the Word there is the truth of receiving all from the Source, the Father. In the human consciousness of Jesus, joined to that Word, there is the human awareness of human limitation. Yet, because the sacred humanity is without sin, there is no shame at being humanly limited. Instead, the sacred humanity rests in the Divinity, and the Divine carries the humanness, manifesting the exquisite beauty of a weaned child. We hear the Word telling us we too must become as a little child.

We realize that of ourselves *we are not.*[9] Shocking to our sensibilities at first hearing, the truth of this reality can create a fine-tuned sense of proportion for our modern sense of what is owed us by right. The truth that of ourselves we are not, that we do not exist, pops the bubble of an overinflated sense of ego in our lives. For someone without a relationship to the Divine, this truth can plunge the consciousness into

---

same sound . . . the small chords of the body's senses and organs are blended. . . . Every member does the work given it to do, each one perfect in its own way: the eye in seeing, the ear in hearing, the nose in smelling, the taste in tasting, the tongue in speaking, the hands in touching and working, the feet in walking. All are harmonized in one sound to serve their neighbors." Catherine of Siena, *The Dialogue*, trans. Suzanne Noffke, OP (New York: Paulist, 1980), 310.

[9] "Do you know, daughter, who you are and who I am? If you know these two things you have beatitude in your grasp. You are she who is not, and I am the one who is. Let your soul become penetrated with this truth, and the Enemy can never lead you astray." Raymond of Capua, *The Life of Catherine of Siena*, trans. Conleth Kearns (Wilmington, DE: Michael Glazier, 1980), 86.

darkest nihilism. But for one in relation to the Divine through faith, the self is known as a worded being, one spoken into existence by the One who is. Then the gift of fear makes perfect sense, and so does the moderation of the longings of the sense appetite. The sense of proportion this beatitude brings is the ordered beauty of truth's goodness.

"Beautiful are those who mourn, for they will be comforted." Tears are the sign of what we hold most valuable.[10] The Word in our humanness wept over Jerusalem (Luke 19:41). In his humanness Jesus knew what it felt like to hit the brick wall of human denial and resistance, and in human frustration he wept. We know the feeling. It can suck the soul into the vortex of despair. Thomas relates this beatitude to the theological virtue of hope and the gift of knowledge. This would have the beauty of this mourning flow from the depths of the desire of the spontaneous emotions of the psyche. Grieving the suffering of the innocent or helpless, the Spirit's own groaning in the soul can be felt for that which is not yet realized. In the unfolding of earth's time, place, and space, there is unfinished business. It is the grieving ache of what is not, in the light of *what could be.*

"Beautiful are the meek, for they will inherit the earth." Meek is not weak. There is no weakness in the silent Jesus before Pilate, in the glance at Peter as Jesus was being led away. Meekness is the capacity to control fury. Anger or fury arises due to threat. I am furious because my dignity or control is threatened, whether that dignity be the destruction of my good name, or that control be of my car on the road, of my prestige on the job, or of my relationship with my wife. The meek know who they are and that they are not in control of anything. This frees them from the emotional roller coaster of the frantic. They use their energy instead to work a situation through. The turf they will possess is the concrete situation in which they stand. They operate from a firm center, not tossed about by the shifting sands of circumstance. Aquinas relates this beatitude to the virtue of religion under justice, and he suggests its assisting gift is piety. The grounding of the soul in

[10] "There is a weeping of fire, of true holy longing, and it consumes in love. Such a soul would like to dissolve her life in weeping in self-contempt and for the salvation of souls, but she seems unable to do it. I tell you, these souls have tears of fire. In this fire the Holy Spirit weeps in my presence for them and for their neighbors. I mean that my divine charity sets ablaze with its flame the soul who offers me her restless longing without any physical tears. These, I tell you, are tears of fire, and this is how the Holy Spirit weeps." Catherine of Siena, *The Dialogue*, 169.

God is a grounding in an identity that cannot be shattered by human injustice and the violation of human rights. It identifies the primary human relationship in God, from which all other relationships flow.

"Beautiful are those who hunger and thirst for righteousness [justice], for they will be filled." The longing evident here is unavoidable. But it is not the longing of simple spontaneous desire or even of considered hope. It is the focused, strong longing of courage. This hunger and thirst has an object, and its desire is manifesting the staying power of fortitude. This desire is in the struggle for the long term and won't quit until there are results to show. In the incarnate Word we find the desire to cast fire upon the earth (cf. Luke 12:49). In us this fire fuses justice with charity, no longer permitting handouts without addressing the structures that keep people's hands out. Thomas would have this beatitude flow from fortitude—both the virtue and the gift, which would manifest the psychic energy transformed, in particular the ordering of the considered emotions because they impact choice.

"Beautiful are the merciful, for they will receive mercy." Mercy is more than kindness. It is kindness in the face of injury. You should get it in the teeth, and I refrain from doling it out back to you. It is not hard to see this beauty active in the Word in the final moments of crucifixion in his words of forgiveness. But what we miss is the prolonged mercy that puts up with the bungling of the Twelve and still puts up with the sinfulness of the church. Thomas has this beatitude flow from the virtue of prudence and the gift of counsel. Perhaps this beauty has to do with judgment, that stage of prudence that has us reach a conclusion about the facts of a situation. It faces us with the fact that we don't have the facts—at least about the motives of those who have injured us. We really don't know their intent any more than others know ours when we goof. How could they possibly know when we don't, when we can only regret our foolishness. Mercy is compassion in the light of the partial truth that prudence has and out of love giving someone the benefit of the doubt that there may be more to this than I know.

"Beautiful are the pure in heart, for they will see God." The pure in heart have a magnificent obsession. They have their eyes on a target and will not be deterred. The pure in heart know they are nothing without God. Like a laser, their intent is focused. They will get exactly what they want. The Word indeed was obsessed: with the will of the Father and the coming of the reign of God (cf. John 4:34; 5:30). He did his Father's will and still yearns to see the reign arrive throughout the earth. For the human, this beatitude reveals a centered and focused life, one not only aware of relationship with the Divine but intent upon grasping it. This beatitude exudes the fragrance of a contemplative consciousness, a gaze on the one thing necessary in the midst of life's ebb and flow. Thomas relates this particular blessedness to the theological virtue of faith strengthened by the gift of understanding. Faith, like a laser, spots the target, and love brings the understanding of the Word that can come only from loving.

"Beautiful are the peacemakers, for they will be called children of God." Peacemakers are reconcilers, and that is what the Word is. The incarnate Word is a bridge, reconciling estranged, broken humanness with the Divine.[11] Those who seek peace are kin to this Word-Son. They bind up the world. Thomas relates this beatitude to the theological virtue of charity and its gift of wisdom. Wise and loving peace seeking is evidence of the Spirit's activity anywhere it is found. This may become a new starting place for reconsidering the activity of grace and the presence of the Spirit in peoples we have considered unbelievers. Where there is evidence of active love, there is the Spirit of God, there is grace. It is the work of the Spirit to bring forth the Word. In the past some have often looked first for explicit commitment to Christ, the explicit presence of the Word, for salvation. What are we to do when there is evidence of the Spirit's presence and, to our knowledge, no explicit confession of Christ? We forget that it is in the Spirit's love that the Word is begotten. What form is the Word taking that I might not recognize because I have my set notion of how he should make his appearance?

"Beautiful are those who are persecuted for righteousness' sake, for theirs is the kingdom of heaven." This beatitude is not related by Thomas to any particular growth in the human. Rather, it points to a condition to be expected in the face of those who don't like the sound of your song or the fragrance you bring. The human healed is a thorn to the human resisting the onslaught of God. Bias is a defense, a protection of the meager knowledge one has, and a fear of new truth. If I know the full truth, it might set me free, and I don't know whether I want to be responsible for such freedom. Veiled, the beauty of the human waits, concealed.

[11] "I told you that I have made a bridge of the Word, my only begotten Son, . . . so that you could cross over the river. . . . It stretches from heaven to earth by reason of my having joined myself with your humanity, which I formed from the earth's clay." Catherine of Siena, *The Dialogue*, 58, 59, 64.

Virtue, gift, fruit, beatitude—no longer mere words, but the naming of divine intervention and human beauty. We are now able to make some distinctions, and these distinctions can be meaningful to those among us guiding the spiritual journeys of others. The power to choose courageously is given (infused virtue of fortitude), and the human chooses to act upon it (emotion of courage aided by the acquired virtue of fortitude), strengthened by the Spirit (gift of fortitude). The result may surprise even us (fruits of patience and long-suffering) as we wonder how we were able to get through thus and so. The blessedness and fragrance of such a life spills out into the community in the beatitude evidence that is right before our eyes if we but know what to look for. The Divine and the human are relationally engaged in creating a new result. The human consciousness, under the influence of the Divine, has created something new. Something beautiful is there to show for it.

Such a person does not *have* a ministry. Such a person *is ministerial in anything he or she does.* The fruit and fragrance of this blessed interplay will nourish the community even from the bed of one paralyzed. This is the heart of true ministry, a ministry first of fruitful *being,* a "real presence." A ministry of fruitful doing may then follow. Authentic formation for ministry begins and ends here. What is brought to the common community table of the Eucharist is first the stuff of the human struggle. It is offered with the hope that what is being summoned forth in me will come to be. When I leave, what leaves with me to mingle in the community is that same human, transformed by the blessedness of divine contact into just a little more beauty.

Nourishing the Beauty: Forgiveness and Prayer

The beauty that is human authenticity is nourished by liturgy, by sacrament, by art, by music, by human relatedness. The consciousness drinks in what it needs. The Divine empowers and purifies in the midst of the ordinary. In the midst of this plethora of nourishments that feed soul making, I single out two: forgiveness and prayer. Forgiveness I liken to a flushing out of the soul, an intentional release of toxins that could make us incapable of the nourishment that prayer is. Prayer is coming before divine Love, clothed in nothing but faith, drawn by hope's aching desire, and breathless on love's bare feet. Unforgiveness covers the ground with shards of broken glass.

Living things can be poisoned and their growth halted altogether. Almost as bad, a living thing can be blighted, its growth crippled, twisted, and deformed. Negatively, forgiveness is the purging that is absolutely necessary for spiritual growth. Jesus was not kidding about forgiving seventy-seven times. If unforgiveness is present in consciousness, it will prevent the nourishment of the soul. It will cripple attempts at prayer. Why is this so?

Forgiveness takes love's temperature. Low, the love is cool; high, the love is warm and real. Without forgiveness, love languishes in the never-never land of the lukewarm. With forgiveness, love holds no prisoners and as a result is itself free. We free our prisoners not because they are not guilty. We free them because to hold them poisons our own souls.

An allegory may help. The entrance to one's deepest core, one's heart, is a gate likened in the Song of Songs to a lovely latticework. The gate of welcome and admittance swings freely in and out. There is no blockage, no barrier. But when there is unforgiveness, the wrought-iron latticework at the entrance of the heart reconfigures itself into a jail cell. There is great satisfaction and an intoxicating sense of power in unforgiveness. We stride around the cell, the key on its ring twirling around our accusing finger. We have our offender tucked away, and he or she is not getting out. Unforgiveness is a subtle form of revenge; now it's our turn.

The toxicity of unforgiveness leeches its way into the soil of our humanness, contaminating the ground water from which our love seeks to draw. There is such satisfaction in getting even by keeping bound one who has hurt us. It feels so right, this getting even. Yet something is wrong with this picture. Shouldn't I feel elated? Then why am I depressed?

Buried unforgiveness is like a toxic dump. Unsuspecting hikers travel in the location and wonder why they feel ill when they get home. The unsuspecting pilgrim needs to check often for the unfinished business of unforgiveness. Nothing is more lethal to love. What are we to do when it is clear we are holding someone hostage?

Active imaging can be very helpful to bring into consciousness what has long been buried and forgotten. The psychic memory needs to be healed, and active imaging can confront the consciousness with what it would rather avoid. But imaging also needs to bring healing. We might picture an image of the risen Christ with the wounds of his victimization clearly visible. Seeking entry with us into the home of our heart, he finds the way blocked by the jail cell of unforgiveness. The heart's door is blocked. The offender will wield continuing power over the victim's memory, which rehashes the injury over and over. The risen One holds out a wounded hand, requesting not only the key but custody of the prisoner. The click of the key must be felt more than heard, the jail cell door swung open, and the prisoner released into this One's custody for truly just handling. Empty, the cell reconfigures itself into a gate of welcome, barring no one.

Forgiveness is a form of divestiture. It peels from love the last vestiges of arrogance, of control over another. Without forgiveness, love is making believe. With forgiveness, love rings true.

With forgiveness clearing the way, prayer also nourishes beauty. Much is written about prayer. Communal prayer takes various forms, from the rich sacramental celebrations of liturgical traditions to the stillness of Quaker sitting. Personal prayer can engage the body through voice and dance, with words, song, and movement. The psyche can be engaged in guided imagery. The intelligence can be focused in reflective meditation. The intentionality of the consciousness can be simply focused on the Divine with helpless longing. There is Scripture-based prayer, the rich framework of the Ignatian Spiritual Exercises, the exuberance of charismatic prayer, and the prayer of quiet. It is clear that one aspect of prayer is that it is something one *does*.

Prayer is also something one *is*. It is coming as one is and being who one is with another. It is being intimate with the Holy. It is being full of tears, spilling over with compassion with those who grieve. It is being in communion with a groaning world. Praying is something the Divine is about secretly in the soul without it being aware. Prayer is sitting in darkness and letting divine Love have its way with a cluttered consciousness. Contemplative consciousness is modeled for us by the child. Crouched over, eyes wide with wonder, the child watches intently while the ants file in and out of the anthill on the sidewalk. This attentive wonder can be turned to more than ants on the sidewalk. Mystical differentiation of consciousness is a developed human awareness of the Divine present in the horizon of our consciousness. *It is an ongoing way to be.* Clothed in nothing but the homespun of faith, we turn our soul's face to the Son, like sunflowers standing in a field. Our soul stands on tiptoe, face uplifted, lips all puckered up, waiting to be kissed. Prayer that has become a differentiation of consciousness can become a constant posture of the soul. Contemplative consciousness is what we are made for. It is a differentiation of consciousness that is brought about by the refinement of loving. It is something one becomes, as surely as a log, at long last, becomes the fire that engulfs it. When prayer becomes more than who one is, than what one does, mystical differentiation of consciousness becomes the capstone of the beautiful person. Like the aesthetic differentiation of consciousness that characterizes the pianist, or a scholarly differentiation of consciousness that marks the scholar, mystical differentiation of consciousness points to holiness at work in the human. It is being touched by the Holy. It is a humble welcome, a making space for God. The transformation caused by *deification* is at work. Human beauty is the result.

Prayer is intensely personal, more personal than one's sexual activity. The more one moves from the doing stage to the prayer that begins to pervade the consciousness, the more difficult it becomes to talk of prayer. The stages of this growth are recounted by masters of the spiritual life. What is of importance for us in this brief consideration is to realize that contemplative consciousness is open to everyone. Not dependent on technique or cleverness, it is developed by desire and love and is often found highly developed among uneducated, humble people. When it is developed it will make one a formidable minister, often pointing the ministry in the direction of the *prophetic*, with all the persecution that comes with it. Because Love is at work in us, we might find ourselves drafted into a role we didn't plan for ourselves. It might be *priestly* self-sacrifice poured out in coping with false accusation. It might be the regal and *royal* dignity we see in the dying who amaze their nurses, or in the faithful janitors who go about their cleanup day after day, or the friendly cabbies who manage to make a living haunting airports and trying to scare up passengers.

The Divine is in relentless pursuit of the human. The human, captivated yet terrified, is always running off yet hoping to be caught. Like a sophisticated game of hide-and-seek, the game goes on. Never tiring of our childishness, the Divine pursues and waits as we come bounding around the corner of yet another pipe dream. We need to come of age, to grow up to be a child. That aging is the maturing of our loving. The loving comes about in the integration of spirituality's foundations, human and divine. The result is the human clothed in beauty. It is the weaving of the wedding garment.

Summary

1. Authentic humanness is beautiful to behold. The result of the Divine's action in the human is the beautiful human being. *Beauty is the observable flow of intelligent choice in the unblocked psychic energy of a person at home in his or her own physicality.*

2. Human beauty is far from an abstraction. It is the concrete result of divine/human interaction and is evident in behavior. Behavior that is not only pleasing but beautiful shows evidence of the *fruits of the Holy Spirit*; it demonstrates concrete charity, joy, peace, patience, benignity (mildness, gentleness, goodness, or kindness), generosity, faithfulness, long-suffering (longanimity), and self-control (modesty, continence, and chastity).

3. The *Beatitudes* are characteristics of the state of a human who is evidencing the transformation that deification brings about. This human beauty brings a distinct tone or fragrance of presence to the world. The distinct presence of such a person is one of holiness. The Beatitudes are evidence of the fruitfulness of holiness in a human life. They are the integrated summation, the tone or fragrance, of a life permeated and responsive to the Divine.

4. *Forgiveness* is a necessity if love is to be authentic. Unforgiveness is toxic to human holiness and destructive of human health. Forgiveness is the decision to release to Love those who have injured us, thus keeping no one held hostage, even in psychic feeling memory.

5. *Prayer* is a form of relationship with the Divine. It may take one of the many forms familiar in the Christian community. The heart of prayer is intimacy with the Holy and often takes the form of a simple focused attentiveness and wonder that can grow to permeate the consciousness in an ever-growing constancy.

6. A consciousness *mystically* differentiated is a consciousness permeated by a semipermanent state of prayer. This kind of developed attentiveness is the birthright of every human being. It is developed by frequent loving attentiveness rather than by any one technique. Concretely aware, intelligent and reasonable, responsible and forgiving, prayerful and full of laughter and tears at the very wonder of existence—such a human being is the trophy of grace's love affair with the human being.

Conclusion

Any text that attempts to provide a framework for the study of spirituality does so knowing the effort must be but a beginning. This work is just such a beginning. I am open to the suggestions of all who read it and can clarify what it attempts to present.

Using the lens of a Christian theotic viewpoint as it does, this study has also been aware that not all share that viewpoint. Nonetheless, the theotic viewpoint is the lens of millions of believers and can give them an anthropological bridge on which to stand while they try to speak about their perspective to those of another viewpoint. I hope that the human foundations discussed here will be of some use to speak to those in the sciences as well, for we all live in a world of sense data and carry on our spiritual pilgrimage there.

Most challenging for believers in a secular age, however, is the premise presented here that the human cannot be considered in isolation apart from the Divine, that to do so would be to violate its very identity. This premise cannot be proven. It can only be believed. In asserting it, I align myself with those who reverence the world of science, for all of us live our lives primarily within a trustful faith. We take the word of others. We follow hunches. We are convinced that the physical world has an important word for us, yet not the last word. In taking a *religious* faith position, I simply acknowledge a dimension *beyond* the empirical. I stand alongside the unbeliever who also chooses a stand. For the unbeliever "real" means "empirically observable." We differ. Each of us, the believer and the unbeliever, must decide how we want to risk.

As a final word in this study, I would like to emphasize directly what may have come through only between the lines. *The spirituality needed in our day is one that gives an account of the operations of the human as well as the activity of the Divine.* No longer can we settle for works on spirituality that emphasize only the one or the other as adequate. *The spirituality of the future will need to bridge the human and the Holy in a way that keeps open the dialogue of the wider ecumenism.* The human, with its consciousness and its distinct spiritual operations, is the common ground on which we all stand. Religious experience is an experience that takes place in human consciousness in whatever culture. Intentionality analysis or some more adequate means of accounting for human functioning must provide an accountability not only for results but for the very *process* the subject uses to arrive at the judgments accepted as true, or judgments of worth or value. We need a communal way of holding one another accountable for our lack of awareness, for our repression of honest questioning, for our rash judgments, and for our resulting rash decisions. At present we excuse ourselves from this task, begging cultural difference. Yet it is this precise malfunctioning of the human that keeps us paralyzed from rejoicing in the truth that is real. We settle for the wayside shrines of our own constructs. We worship in our own egoisms and take offense when we are reminded that we must be on our way to the temple.

Even more critical in our time is the need for a meaningful way to speak of the Holy. I suspect it follows in the face of first allowing the human to have its say. Who is it we are addressing? Who calls us to be holy? Who is it to whom we are attempting to respond?

Spirituality is like the genie let out of the bottle. It is not going back in. It remains for us to give an account and to provide a methodology for discussing this constitutive dimension of the human being in a way that respects religious experience worldwide. It is the basic assumption of this study that the most basic methodology for this and other pursuits is first an attentiveness to the operations of our own consciousness as it experiences, understands, judges, and then decides. It is my hope that this study has made a tentative beginning in that direction, drawing from the perspective of the Catholic Christian tradition while remaining open to the outer manifestations of other traditions. I remain convinced that it is only in the inner core, in the universality of religious experience and the human operations of experience, understanding, judgment, and decision, that we find the common ground that unifies us. It is in this inner core that spirituality provides the sanctuary for the plurality of diverse faith traditions to flourish and to find the strength to purify themselves as they move through history celebrating their richness.

Diagram 1

A Sketch of Human Anthropology and Human Emotion

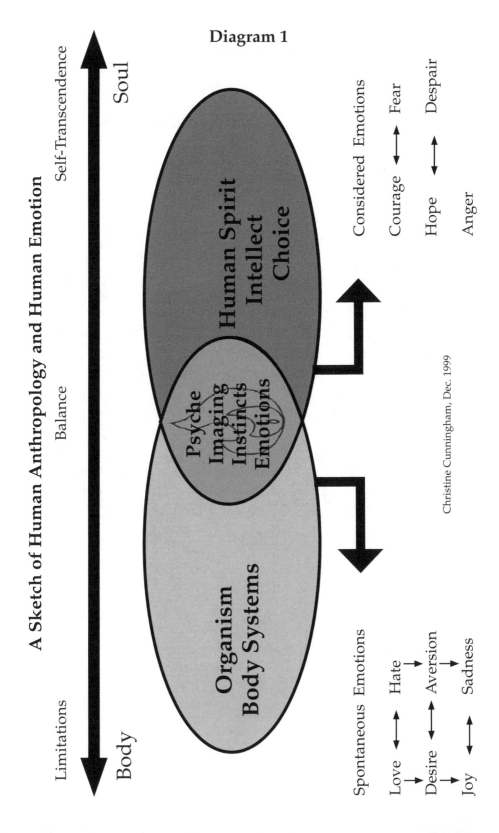

Christine Cunningham, Dec. 1999

Diagram 2

The Dynamic Human Consciousness

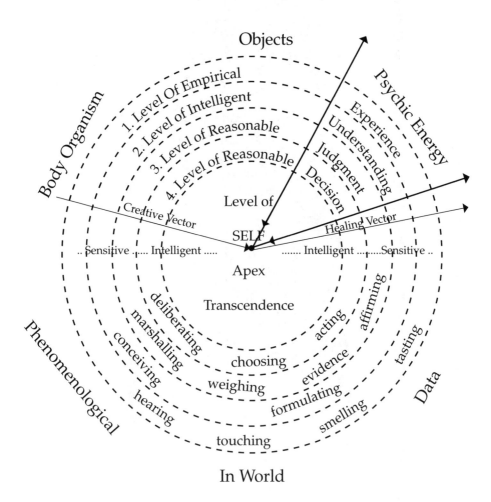

Christine Cunningham, Dec. 1999

Diagram 3

At the center of my being is a point of pure nothingness which is untouched by sin and by illusion, a point of pure truth, a point or spark which belongs entirely to God, which is never at our disposal, from which God disposes of our lives, which is inaccessible to the fantasies of our own mind or the brutalities of our own will. This little point of nothingness and of absolute poverty is the pure glory of God in us.

—Thomas Merton,
Conjectures of a Guilty Bystander
(New York: Doubleday, 1966), 142

The Center (Apex) of Human Consciousness

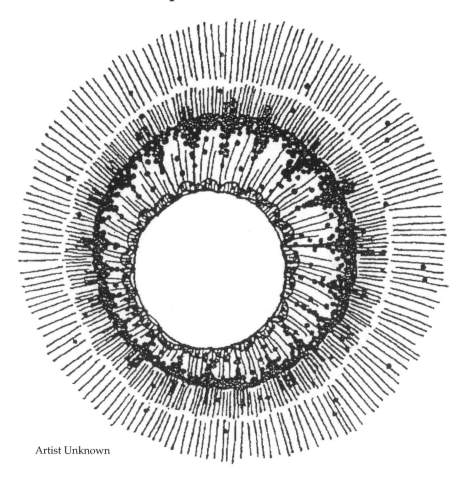

Artist Unknown

General Bibliography

Allchin, A. M. "The Self Transformed: The Rediscovery of a Doctrine." *The Way* 30:2 (April 30, 1990): 135–47.

Amrhein, Eva Maria, and Robert A. Brungs, SJ. "The Task of Christians in Science." In *The Vineyard: Scientists in the Church*. St. Louis: ITEST Faith/Science Press, 1992.

Aquinas, Thomas. *Summa Theologiae*. Blackfriars Edition. 61 vols. New York: McGraw and Hill, 1964–81.

Arbuckle, Gerald A., and David L. Fleming, eds. *Religious Life: Rebirth through Conversion*. Staten Island, NY: Alba House, 1990.

Arnold, Johann Christof. "The Deeds of Mercy." *The Plough Reader* (Spring 2000): 3–6.

Arnold, Patrick M. "In Search of the Hero: Masculine Spirituality and Liberal Christianity." *America* (October 7, 1989): 206–10.

Au, Wilkie. "Sexuality in the Service of Life and Love." In *By Way of the Heart*, 147–67. New York/Mahwah: Paulist, 1989.

Baars, Conrad W. "Emotions—Man's [*sic*] Psychological Motors" and "How Our Psychological Motors Run." In *Feeling and Healing Your Emotions: A Christian Psychiatrist Shows You How to Grow to Wholeness*, 11–37 and 57–78. Plainfield, NJ: Logos International, 1979.

Barr, Stephen M. Review of *The Quantum Brain: The Search for Freedom and the Next Generation of Man*, by Jeffrey Satinover. *First Things* (November 2001): 43–46.

Barry, William A., and Kerry Maloney, eds. *A Hunger for God: Ten Approaches to Prayer*. Kansas City, MO: Sheed and Ward, 1991.

Bechtle, Regina. "Theological Trends: Convergence in Theology and Spirituality." *The Way* 23 (1985): 305–14.

Berry, Thomas. *The Dream of the Earth*. San Francisco: Sierra Club Books, 1988.

Best-Selling Spirituality: American Cultural Change and the New Shape of Faith. Powhatan, VA: Mars Hill Audio, 1999.

Billy, Dennis J. "Growing in the Virtues and the Gifts: Spiritual Direction as a Practical Theological Locus for the Convergence of Spirituality and Morality." *Studia Moralia* 39:2 (2001): 433–59.

Bouchard, Charles. "The Gifts of the Holy Spirit and Adult Morality." *Liguorian* (May–June 2000): 16–19.

———. "Recovering the Gifts of the Holy Spirit in Moral Theology." *Theological Studies* 63 (2002): 539–58.

Bouyer, Louis. *Introduction to Spirituality*. Collegeville, MN: Liturgical Press, 1961.

Brennan, Robert Edward. *General Psychology: A Study of Man Based on St. Thomas Aquinas*. New York: Macmillan, 1952.

Brown, Neil. *Spirit of the World: The Moral Basis of Christian Spirituality*. Sydney: The Catholic Institute, 1990.

Brown, Robert McAffe. *Spirituality and Liberation: Overcoming the Great Fallacy*. Philadelphia: Westminster Press, 1988.

Brown, Wareen S., Nancey Murphy, and Malony H. Newton, eds. *Whatever Happened to the Soul? Scientific and Theological Portraits of Human Nature*. Minneapolis: Fortress, 1998.

Byrne, Lavinia, ed. *Traditions of Spiritual Guidance*. Collegeville, MN: Liturgical Press, 1990.

Callahan, Annice. "The Relation between Spirituality and Theology." *Horizons* 16:2 (1989): 266–74.

Callahan, William. *Noisy Contemplation: Deep Prayer for Busy People* (Hyattsville, MD: Quixote Center, 1994 [rev. ed., Brentwood, MD: Quixote Center, 2008]).

———. *The Wind Is Rising: Prayer Ways for Active People* (Mt. Rainier, MD: Quixote Center, 1978).

Campell, Peter A., and Edwin M. McMahon. *Bio-Spirituality: Focusing as a Way to Grow*. Chicago: Loyola University Press, 1985.

Cantwell, Peter W. "Ongoing Growth through Intimacy." *Human Development* 2:3 (Fall 1981): 14–20.

Capra, Fritjof, and David Steindle-Rast, with Thomas Matus. *Belonging to the Universe: Explorations on the Frontiers of Science and Spirituality*. San Francisco: Harper, 1991.

Carey, Raymond P. "Psychosexuality and the Development of Celibacy Skills." *Seminary News* 31:1 (September 1992): 18–24.

Carmody, Denise L. "The Desire for Transcendence: Religious Conversion." In Gregson, ed., *The Desires of the Human Heart*, 57–73.

Catherine of Siena. *The Dialogue*. Suzanne Noffke, OP, trans. New York: Paulist, 1980.

Cessario, Romanus. "What Is a Moral Virtue?" "Prudence and the Moral Virtues," and "What Causes the Moral Virtues to Develop?" In *The Moral Virtues and Theological Ethics*, 45–71, 72–93, and 94–125. Notre Dame, IN: University of Notre Dame Press, 1991.

Collins, Pat. *Intimacy and the Hungers of the Heart*. Mystic, CT: Twenty-Third Publications, 1991.

Collins, Patrick W. "Integrated Sexuality will Re-Shape Church in 21st Century." *Churchwatch* (April–May 1995): 4–6.

Conn, Walter E. *Christian Conversion: A Developmental Interpretation of Autonomy and Surrender*. New York/Mahwah: Paulist, 1986.

———. "Christian Conversion: The Moral Dimension." In *Christian Conversion*, 158–211.

———. "Conversion: A Developmental Perspective," *Cross Currents* 32 (1982): 323–28.

———. "The Desire for Authenticity: Conscience and Moral Conversion." In Gregson, ed., *The Desires of the Human Heart*, 36–56.

———. "Moral Development: Is Conversion Necessary?" In Matthew Lamb, ed., *Creativity and Method*, 307–24.

———. "Two-Handed Theology." *Proceedings of the Catholic Theological Society of America* 38 (1983): 66–71.

Cousins, Ewert. "Spirituality for the New Axial Period." *Christian Spirituality Bulletin* (Fall 1994): 12–15.

Cox, Michael. *Handbook of Christian Spirituality: A Guide to Figures and Teachings from the Biblical Era to the Twentieth Century*. San Francisco: Harper and Row, 1985.

Cronin, Brian. "Religious and Christian Conversion in an African Context." *African Christian Studies* 3:2 (June 1987): 19–35.

Crosby, Michael H. "The Relevance of Matthew's Gospel" and "Whose Is the Reign of God?" In *Spirituality of the Beatitudes: Matthew's Challenge for First World Christians*, 1–24 and 25–48. Maryknoll, NY: Orbis, 1981.

Daly, Thomas V. "Consciousness and the Human Spirit." *Journal of Clinical Neuroscience* 3:2 (April 1996): 114–17.

D'Aquili, Eugene, and Andrew B. Newberg. *The Mystical Mind: Probing the Biology of Religious Experience*. Minneapolis: Fortress, 1999.

De Sousa, Ronald. *The Rationality of Emotion*. Cambridge, MA: MIT Press, 1987.

Doran, Robert M. "Consciousness and Grace." *Method: Journal of Lonergan Studies* 11 (1993): 51–75.

———. "From Psychic Conversion to the Dialectic of Community." *Lonergan Workshop* 6 (1986): 85–106.

———. "Jung and Catholic Theology." In J. Marvin Spiegelman, ed., *Catholicism and Jungian Psychology*, 41–73. Phoenix, AZ: Falcon Press, 1988.

———. "Jungian Psychology and Christian Spirituality," Parts 1, 2, and 3. *Review for Religious* (July 1979): 497–510; (September 1979): 742–52; and (November 1979): 857–66.

———. "Psychic Conversion." *The Thomist* (1977): 200–36.

————. "Soul-Making and the Opposites." In *Psychic Conversion and Theological Foundations: Toward a Reorientation of the Human Sciences*, 139–54, parts 1, 3, and 5. Chico, CA: Scholars Press, 1981.

————. *Theology and the Dialectics of History*. Toronto: University of Toronto Press, 1990.

Dowd, Michael. *Earthspirit: A Handbook for Nurturing an Ecological Christianity*. Mystic, CT: Twenty-Third Publications, 1991.

Downey, Michael. "The Changing Terrain of Christian Spirituality." *Praying* (September–October 1993): 30–31, 44.

————. "Christian Spirituality: Changing Currents, Perspectives, Challenges." *America* (April 2, 1994): 8–12.

————, ed. "Creation Spirituality: Presentation and Challenge." *Listening: Journal of Religion and Culture* 24:2 (Spring 1989).

Dreyer, Elizabeth A. "The Importance of Being Sorry." *U.S. Catholic* (August 1998): 18–23.

Driscoll, Jeremy. "The Psalms and Psychic Conversion." *Cistercian Studies* 22 (1987): 91–110.

Drost, Mark P. "In the Realm of the Senses: Saint Thomas Aquinas on Sensory Love, Desire, and Delight." *The Thomist* 59:1 (January 1995): 47–58.

Drummond, Thomas B. "Intimacy: What It Is and What It Ain't." *New Life Center Newsletter* (Summer 1993): 1, 3, 7, 9, 13, and 19.

Dudley, Glenn G. *Infinity and the Brain: A Unified Theory of Mind, Matter, and God*. St. Paul, MN: Paragon House, 2002.

Dunne, Tad. "Consciousness in Christian Community." In Matthew Lamb, ed., *Creativity and Method*, 291–303.

————. "Faith, Charity, and Hope." *Lonergan Workshop* 5 (1985): 49–70.

————. *Lonergan and Spirituality: Towards a Spiritual Integration*. Chicago: Loyola University Press, 1985.

————. *We Cannot Find Words: The Foundations of Prayer*. Denville, NJ: Dimension Books, 1981.

Egan, Harvey D. *Christian Mysticism: The Future of a Tradition*. New York: Pueblo, 1984.

————. "The Christian Mystics and Today's Theological Horizon." *Listening: Journal of Religion and Culture* (Autumn 1982): 203–15.

————. *What Are They Saying about Mysticism?* New York: Paulist, 1982.

Egan, John. "The Christian Mystics and Today's Theological Horizon." *Listening: Journal of Religion and Culture* (Autumn 1982): 203–15.

Eidle, William R. "Interiority: Intentionality," "Symbol Forming Psyche," and "Self, Subject, and Person: A Lonerganian Perspective." In *The Self-Appropriation of Interiority: A Foundation for Psychology*, 13–38, 51–68, and 85–101. New York: Peter Lang, 1990.

Eigo, Francis A., ed. *The Human Experience of Conversion: Persons and Structures in Transformation*. Villanova, PA: Villanova University Press, 1987.

Faricy, Robert. "Henri de Lubac: Scripture's Meaning for Prayer." In *Praying*, 85–98. Minneapolis: Winston Press, 1979.

Fatula, Mary Ann. "Our Inner Teacher" and "Intimate Friendship with the Holy Spirit." In *The Holy Spirit: Unbounded Gift of Joy*, 121–32 and 147–60. Collegeville, MN: Liturgical Press, 1998.

Finley, James. *Merton's Palace of Nowhere: A Searching for God through Awareness of the True Self*. Notre Dame: Ave Maria Press, 1978.

Forest, James. *The Ladder of the Beatitudes*. Maryknoll, NY: Orbis, 1999.

———. "Waking from a Dream." *The Catholic Worker* LV:8 (December 1988): 1 and 8.

Fortenbaugh, W. W. *Aristotle on Emotion*. N.p.: Barnes and Noble, 1975.

Fox, Matthew. "The Body and the Sacred." *Creation* 7:3 (1991).

———. "Is Creation Spirituality 'New Age'?" *Creation* (July–August 1988): 10–11.

———. "Letter to Ratzinger." *Creation* 4:5 (1988).

Frohnhofen, Herbert. "The Holy Spirit: Source, Goal, and Fruit of Our Prayer." *Theology Digest* 71:1 (January–February 1998): 1–10; summary of "Heiliger Geist—Quelle, Ziel und Frucht unseres Gabetes," *Geist und Leben: Zeitschrift für christliche Spiritualität*.

Giardini, Fabio. "The Growth Process of Christian Prayer Life." *Angelicum* 60 (1992): 389–421.

Goergen, Donald. "Calling Forth a Healthy Chaste Life." *Review for Religious* (May–June 1998): 260–74.

Goldbrunner, Josef. "Faith and Depth Psychology." *Worship* 42:1 (1968): 22–30.

Gordon, Robert M. *The Structure of Emotions: Investigations in Cognitive Philosophy*. Cambridge, MA: Cambridge University Press, 1987.

Greeley, Andrew M., and Mary Greeley Durkin. "Sex as Sacramental Experience." In *How to Save the Catholic Church*, 105–29. New York: Viking, 1984.

Greenberg, Leslie S. "Emotions and Change Processes in Psychotherapy." In M. L. Lewis and J. M. Havilan, eds., *Handbook of Emotions*, 499–508.

Greenberg, Leslie S., and Sandra C. Paivo. *Working with Emotions in Psychotherapy*. New York/London: Guilford Press, 1997.

Gregson, Vernon, ed. "The Desire to Know: Intellectual Conversion." In *The Desires of the Human Heart: An Introduction to the Theology of Bernard Lonergan*. New York/Mahwah: Paulist, 1988.

———. "Levels of Consciousness." In *Lonergan, Spirituality, and the Meeting of World Religions*, 29–58. Lanham, MD: University Press of America, 1985.

Guroian, Vigen. "The Gift of the Holy Spirit: Reflections on Baptism and Growth in Holiness." *Studies in Christian Ethics* 12:1 (April 1999): 23–34.

Hamm, Dennis. *Beatitudes in Context*. Collegeville, MN: Liturgical Press, 1990.

Hanson, Bradley C. "What Is Spirituality?" In *Modern Christian Spirituality: Methodological and Historical Essays*, 15–61. Atlanta: Scholars Press, 1990.

Happel, Stephen. "Sacrament: Symbol of Conversion." In Matthew Lamb, ed., *Creativity and Method*, 275–89.

————. "The Sacraments: Symbols That Redirect Our Desires." In Gregson, ed., *Desires of the Human Heart*, 237–54.

Harak, G. Simon. *Virtuous Passions: The Formation of Christian Character*. New York/Mahwah: Paulist, 1993.

Hardon, John A. "Meaning of Virtue in St. Thomas Aquinas." *The Catholic Faith* 1:1 (September–October 1995): 29–33.

Helminiak, Daniel A. "The Theotic Viewpoint." In *Religion and the Human Sciences: An Approach via Spirituality*. New York: SUNY, 1998.

Hillman, James. "Peaks and Vales: The Soul/Spirit Distinction as Basis for the Differences between Psychotherapy and Spiritual Discipline." In J. Needleman and D. Lewis, eds., *On the Way to Self-Knowledge*, 54–73. New York: Knopf, 1976.

James, William. "What Is an Emotion?" *Mind: A Quarterly Review of Psychology and Philosophy* 9 (1884): 188–205.

Johnston, William. *Christian Mysticism Today*. San Francisco: Harper and Row, 1984.

————. *The Inner Eye of Love: Mysticism and Religion*. San Francisco: Harper and Row, 1978.

————. *The Mirror Mind: Spirituality and Transformation*. San Francisco: Harper and Row, 1981.

————. *Silent Music: the Science of Meditation*. San Francisco: Harper and Row, 1974.

————. *The Still Point: Reflections on Zen and Christian Mysticism*. New York: Fordham University Press, 1970.

Jones, Alan. "Spirituality and Theology." *Review for Religious* 39:2 (1980): 161–76.

Jones, Cheslyn, Geoffrey Wainwright, and Edward Yarnold. *The Study of Spirituality*. New York: Oxford University Press, 1986.

Keely, Richard C. "Prayer and Work." In Barry and Moloney, eds., *A Hunger for God*, 117–29.

Kenel, Mary Elizabeth. "A Celibate's Sexuality and Intimacy." *Human Development* 7:1 (Spring 1986): 14–19.

Kereszty, Roch. "Theology and Spirituality: The Task of a Synthesis." *Communio* 10:4 (Winter 1983): 314–31.

Kinberger, Mary Kay. "Conversion." *Spirituality Today* 44:1 (Spring 1989): 42–53.

Kinerk, Edward. "Toward a Method for the Study of Spirituality." *Review for Religious* 40:1 (1981): 3–19.

King, J. Norman. "The Experience of God in the Theology of Karl Rahner." *Thought* 53 (June 1978): 174–202.

————. *Experiencing God All Ways and Every Day*. Minneapolis: Winston Press, 1982.

Klein, Dennis D. "Toxic Shame and the Lonerganian Concept of Conversion." In Peter Vincent Amato Oneonta, ed., *Virtue, Order, Mind: Ancient, Modern, and Post-Modern Perspectives*, 89–103. New York: SUNY, 1994.

LaCentra, Walter. "The Demands of Intellectual Self-Appropriation" and "Moral Freedom and Moral Impotence." In *The Authentic Self: Toward a Philosophy of Personality*, 19–32 and 35–48. New York: Peter Lang, 1987.

Lamb, Matthew, ed. *Creativity and Method*. Milwaukee: Marquette University Press, 1981.

Lampman, Jane. "Scientists Put Love under the Microscope." *Christian Science Monitor* 94:132 (June 3, 2002): 1 and 4.

La Verdiere, Eugene. "Fundamentalism: A Pastoral Concern." Collegeville, MN: Liturgical Press, 2000. Reprint from *The Bible Today* 21:1 (January 1983): 5–11.

Leech, Kenneth. "God in the Flesh." In *Experiencing God: Theology as Spirituality*, 236–64. San Francisco: Harper and Row, 1985.

Levho, John J. "Temptations and Their Relation to Prayer for John Cassian." *Diakonia* (1996): 85–94.

Levin, Jeffrey S. "How Prayer Heals: A Theoretical Model." *Alternative Therapies* 2:1 (January 1996): 66–73.

Lewis, M. L., and J. M. Havilan, eds. *Handbook of Emotions*. New York: Guilford Press, 1993.

Liddy, Richard M. "Theology as Intellectual Conversion." *Proceedings of the Catholic Theological Society of America* 33 (1978): 123–34.

Lonergan, Bernard. *Collected Works of Bernard Lonergan*. Vol. 4, *Collection*. Edited by Frederick E. Crowe and Robert M. Doran. Toronto: University of Toronto Press, 1988.

———. *Collected Works of Bernard Lonergan*. Vol. 3, *Insight: Study of Human Understanding*. Edited by Frederick E. Crowe and Robert M. Doran. Toronto: University of Toronto Press, 1992.

———. *Method in Theology*. London: Darton, Longman and Todd, 1971.

———. *Second Collection*. Edited by William F. J. Ryan and Bernard J. Tyrrell. London: Darton, Longman and Todd, 1974.

Looy, Heather. "Disgust, Morality, and Human Identity: A Neurobiological, Psychosocial, and Theological Investigation." *Metanexus*, December 3, 2001, http://www.metanexus.net.

Louf, Andre. "On Some of the Fruits of the Spirit" and "Growing in Grace through Prayer." In *Tuning in to Grace: The Quest for God*, 109–45. Kalamazoo, MI: Cistercian Publications, 1992.

Louth, Andrew. *The Origins of the Mystical Tradition*. Oxford: Clarendon Press, 1981.

Maas, Robin, and Gabriel O'Donnell. *Spiritual Traditions for the Contemporary Church*. Nashville: Abingdon Press, 1990.

MacKnee, Chuck M. "Sexuality and Spirituality: In Search of Common Ground." *Journal of Psychology and Christianity* 16:3 (1997): 210–21.

MacLean, Paul D. "Cerebral Evolution of Emotion." In M. L. Lewis and J. M. Haviland, eds., *Handbook of Emotions*, 67–83.

Main, John. *The Way of Unknowing: Expanding Spiritual Horizons through Meditation*. New York: Crossroad, 1990.

Maloney, Raymond. "The Person as Subject of Spirituality in the Writings of Bernard Lonergan." *Milltown Studies* 45 (2000): 66–80.

———. "The Spiritual Journey in the Writings of Bernard Lonergan." *Milltown Studies* 46 (2000): 112–27.

Markey, John J. "The 'Problem' of Homosexuality." *New Blackfriars* 75:886 (October 1994): 476–88.

Martos, Joseph. "The Sacraments and Global Spirituality." In *The Catholic Sacraments*, 209–24. Wilmington, DE: Michael Glazier, 1983.

May, Gerald. "Energy: The Unifying Force." In *Will and Spirit: A Contemplative Psychology*, 172–209. San Francisco: HarperSanFrancisco, 1982.

Mazza, Enrico. *Mystagogy: A Theology of Liturgy in the Patristic Age*. New York: Pueblo, 1989.

McCarthy, Charles. "Fr. George Zabelka." *The Catholic Worker* (June–July 1992): 6.

McClory, Robert. "How I Came to Forgive the Unforgivable." *U.S. Catholic* (August 1998): 10–17.

McGinn, Bernard and John Meyendorff, eds. *Christian Spirituality: Origins to the Twelfth Century*. Vol. 16 of *World Spirituality: An Encyclopedic History of the Religious Quest*. New York: Crossroad, 1985.

———. "Mysticism and Sexuality." *The Way* 77 (Summer 1993): 46–54.

McGinty, Mary Peter. *The Sacrament of Christian Life*. Chicago: Thomas Moore Press, 1992.

Meyers, John C. "Whatever Happened to the Cardinal Virtues?" *The Living Light* 32:4 (Summer 1996): 10–16.

Monette, Peter L. "Conversion and the Constitutive Function of Grace." *Science et Esprit* 44:1 (1992): 79–82.

Moore, Sebastian. *The Crucified Is No Stranger*. London: Darton, Longman and Todd, 1977.

———. *The Inner Loneliness*. New York: Crossroad, 1982.

———. *Jesus the Liberator of Desire*. New York: Crossroad, 1989.

———. "The Universe at Prayer: What Does It Mean to Pray?" In Barry and Moloney, eds., *A Hunger for God*, 1–9.

Moore, Thomas. *The Care of the Soul: A Guide for Cultivating Depth and Sacredness in Everyday Life*. New York: HarperCollins, 1992.

Neu, Jerome. *Emotion, Thought and Therapy*. Berkeley: University of California Press, 1997.

Newberg, Andrew, Eugene d'Aquili, and Vince Ruse. *Why God Won't Go Away: Brain Science and the Biology of Belief*. New York: Ballentine, 2001. Five-part commentary on *Metanexus* beginning on December 10, 2001, at http://www.metanexus.net.

Nicholl, Donald. *Holiness*. London: Darton, Longman and Todd, 1981.

Ochs, Robert. *God Is More Present Than You Think: Experiments for Closing the Gap in Prayer*. New York: Paulist, 1970.

O'Malley, William J. "Kindness." *America* (February 14, 1998): 10–16.

O'Meara, Thomas F. "Virtue in the Theology of Thomas Aquinas." *Theological Studies* 58:2 (1997): 254–85.

Ormerod, Neil. "Faith Development: Fowler and Lonergan Revisited." *Method* 15 (1997): 191–208.

O'Shea, Kevin. *The Way of Tenderness*. New York: Paulist, 1978.

Osimo, Catherine. "Women's Center: Incarnational Spirituality." In Nadine Foley, ed., *Claiming Our Truth*, 9–34. Washington, DC: Leadership Conference of Women Religious, 1988.

Patoine, Brenda. "Tracing the Brain Roots of Evil." *Brainwork: The Neuroscience Newsletter* 11:4 (July–August 2001): 1–2.

Pert, Candace B. *Molecules of Emotion: Why You Feel the Way You Feel*. New York: Scribner, 1997.

Pinckaers, Servais. "Virtue Is Not a Habit." *Cross Currents* (Winter 1962): 65–81.

Pitcher, George. "Emotion." *Mind: A Quarterly Review of Psychology and Philosophy* 74 (1965): 326–46.

Porter, Jean. "The Affective Virtues," "Justice,"and "Prudence; Cardinal and Theological Virtues." In *The Recovery of Virtue: The Relevance of Aquinas for Christian Virtue*, 100–71. Louisville, KY: Westminster/John Knox, 1990.

Price, James Robertson. "Conversion and the Doctrine of Grace in Bernard Lonergan and John Climacus." *Angelican Theological Review* 62:4 (October 1980): 338–62.

———. "Lonergan and the Foundation of a Contemporary Mystical Theology." *Lonergan Workshop* 5 (1985): 163–94.

———. "Mystical Analysis and the Possibility of a Contemporary Spiritual Theology." Lecture given in Toronto, the Lonergan Research Institute, 1982.

———. "The Objectivity of Mystical Truth Claims." *The Thomist* 49 (1985): 81–98.

———. "Typologies and the Cross-Cultural Analysis of Mysticism: A Critique." In Timothy P. Fallon, SJ, and Philip Boo Riley, eds., *Essays in Honor of Bernard Lonergan, S.J.*, 181–90. Albany: State University of New York, 1987.

Principe, Walter. *Thomas Aquinas' Spirituality*. Etienne Gilson Series 7. Toronto: Pontifical Institute of Medieval Studies, 1984.

———. "Toward Defining Spirituality." *Studies in Religion/Sciences Religieuses* 12:2 (June 1983): 127–41.

Quesnell, Quentin. "Grace." In Gregson, ed., *The Desires of the Human Heart*, 168–81.

Rahner, Karl. "The Spirit of the Future." In *The Practice of Faith*, 18–26. New York: Crossroad, 1983.

Restak, Richard. *The Secret Life of the Brain*. Washington, DC: The Dana Press/Joseph Henry Press, 2001.

Richards, P. Scott, and Allen E. Bergin. *A Spiritual Strategy for Counseling and Psychotherapy*. Washington, DC: American Psychological Association, 1997.

Ring, Nancy C. "Sin and Transformation from a Systematic Perspective." *Chicago Studies* 23 (1984): 303–19.

Rolheiser, Ronald. *The Holy Longing: The Search for a Christian Spirituality*. New York: Doubleday, 1999.

Ruffing, Janet. "Encountering Love Mysticism." *Presence* 41:1 (January 1995): 20–33.

Sardella, Dennis J. "Thoughts about Science and Prayer." In Barry and Moloney, eds., *A Hunger for God*, 98–116.

Savary, L. M., and P. H. Berne. "Kything." In *Prayerways*, 147–55. Harper and Row, 1980.

Schepers, Maurice. "Discovery of Mind and Psyche in the Development of the Theologian: The Conjunction of Intellectual and Affective Conversions." *African Christian Studies* 7:3 (September 1991): 36–45.

Schineller, Peter. "Tensions of an Incarnational Spirituality." *Spirituality Today* 33:4 (December 1981): 340–55.

Schlitt, Dale. "Toward a New Christian Understanding of Faith, Hope and Love." *Église et Théologie* 20 (1989): 385–406.

Schneiders, Sandra M. *Beyond Patching: Faith and Feminism in the Catholic Church*. New York/Mahwah, NJ: Paulist, 1991.

———. "Celibacy as Charism." *The Way* 77 (Summer 1993): 13–25.

———. "Spirituality in the Academy." *Theological Studies* 50 (1989): 676–97.

———. "The Study of Christian Spirituality: Contours and Dynamics of a Discipline." *Christian Spirituality Bulletin* 6:1 (Spring 1998): 1–12.

———. "Theology and Spirituality: Strangers, Rivals, or Partners?" *Horizons* 13:2 (1986): 253–74.

Sedgwich, Timothy. "Worship and Paschal Identity." In *Sacramental Ethics, Paschal Identity and the Christian Life*, 38–52. Philadelphia: Fortress, 1987.

Sinetar, Marsha. *Ordinary People as Monks and Mystics: Lifestyles for Self-Discovery*. New York/Mahwah: Paulist, 1986.

Smith, Cyprian. "Melting," "The Voice of God," and "The Incarnate Word." In *The Way of Paradox*, 43–57, 58–71, and 72–86. London: Darton, Longman and Todd, 1987.

Smith, Marc E. "Can Moral and Religious Conversion Be Separated?" *Thought* 56 (1981): 178–84.

Smith, Susan W. "Bernard of Clairvaux and the Nature of the Human Being: The Special Senses." *Cistercian Studies Quarterly* 30:1 (1995): 3–13.

Soelle, Dorothee. *The Window of Vulnerability: A Political Spirituality*. Minneapolis: Fortress, 1990.

Solomon, Robert C. "The Philosophy of Emotion." In M. L. Lewis and J. M. Havilan, eds., *Handbook of Emotions*, 3–15.

Staniloae, Dimitri. "The Holy Spirit and the Sobornicity of the Church." In *Theology and Church*, 45–71. Crestwood, NY: St. Vladimir's Seminary Press, 1980.

Streeter, Carla Mae. "A New Song: A Theology of Sexuality." *Symposium*. Spiritual Directors International (February 1998): 1–2.

———. "Aquinas, Lonergan, and the Split Soul." *Theology Digest* 32:4 (Winter 1985): 327–40.

———. "The Gift of Real Presence." *Racine Dominican Vocation Publication* (October 23, 1991, revised 1997): 1–4.

———. "Stirred Up by Desire: The Search for an Incarnational Spirituality." In William P. Loewe and Vernon J. Gregson, eds., *Jesus Crucified and Risen: Essays in Spirituality and Theology in Honor of Dom Sebastian Moore,* 147–59. Collegeville, MN: Liturgical Press, 1998.

———. "On Being Real." *Diotima,* a publication of the College of Saint Benedict, St. Joseph, MN (March 19, 1986): 1–4.

———. "What is Spirituality?" *Review for Religious* 56:5 (September–October 1997): 533–41. A shorter form can be found in *Health Progress* (May/June 1996): 17, 22.

St. Romain, Philip. *Kundalini Energy and Christian Spirituality: A Pathway to Growth and Healing.* New York: Crossroad, 1991.

Thompson, William G. "Spirituality, Spiritual Development, and Holiness." *Review for Religious* 51:5 (September–October 1992): 646–58.

Thompson, William M. "Spirituality's Challenges to Today's Theology." *Josephinum Journal of Theology* 8:1 (Winter/Spring 2001): 54–73.

Todaro-Franceschi, Viddette. *The Enigma of Energy: Where Science and Religion Converge.* New York: Crossroad, 1999.

Tugwell, Simon. *The Beatitudes: Soundings in Christian Traditions.* Springfield, IL: Templegate, 1994.

———. "Saint Thomas Aquinas: On the Spiritual Life." *Listening: Journal of Religion and Culture* 26:3 (Fall 1991): 189–99.

Tyrrell, Bernard J. "The Role of Conversion in the Avoidance of 'Burnout.'" Unpublished manuscript, Lonergan Research Institute, Toronto, 1–35.

Ulanov, Ann and Barry. *The Healing Imagination: The Meeting of Psyche and Soul.* New York/Mahwah: Paulist, 1991.

University of California, Los Angeles. "UCLA Team Maps How Genes Affect Brain Structure, Intelligence." November 5, 2001. http://www.universityofcalifornia .edu/news/article/3698.

Vande Kemp, Hendrika. "Psychology and Christian Spirituality: Explorations of the Inner World." *Journal of Psychology and Christianity* 15:2 (1996): 161–74.

Vanier, Jean. *The Scandal of Service: Jesus Washes Our Feet.* New York: Continuum, 1998.

Van Kaam, Adrian. *Spirituality and the Gentle Life.* Denville, NJ: Dimension Books, 1974.

Wadell, Paul J. "Charity: The Virtue of Friendship with God," "The Passions and Affections in the Moral Life: Exploring the Primacy of Love," "The Passions and Affections in the Moral Life: Finding the Strength to Go On," "The Virtues: Actions to Guide Us to Fullness of Life," and "Finding Our Perfection in a Gift." In *The Primacy of Love: An Introduction to the Ethics of Thomas Aquinas,* 63–153. New York/Mahwah: Paulist, 1992.

Westley, Richard. "We Are Makers of Love." *Call to Action* (June–July 1994): 3–6.

Whitehead, Evelyn and James. *Christian Life Patterns: The Psychological Challenges and Religious Invitations of Adult Life.* New York: Crossroad, 1992.

Wiesner, Theodore. "Experiencing God in the Poor." *Spiritual Life* 33 (Winter 1987): 213–21.

Wimberly, Edward P., and Anne Streaty. *Liberation and Human Wholeness: The Conversion Experience of Black People in Slavery and Freedom.* Nashville: Abingdon Press, 1986.

Wiseman, James A. "Teaching Spiritual Theology: Methodological Reflections." *Spirituality Today* 41 (1989): 143–59.

Woods, Richard. "Homophilia and Homophobia: Gays, Lesbians, and Religious Communities." *Horizon* 20:1 (Fall 1994): 9–14.

———, ed. *Understanding Mysticism.* Garden City, NY: Doubleday, 1980.

Index